MAIOLICA VASE
Polychrome Decoration, Showing Spanish Influence
Made in Puebla, Mexico, About 1780

Art Handbook

of the

Pennsylvania Museum and School of Industrial Art

The Maiolica

of

Mexico

by

EDWIN ATLEE BARBER, A.M., PH.D.

Director

Author of

"Pottery and Porcelain of the United States"
"Anglo-American Pottery"
"American Glassware, Old and New"
"Tulip Ware of the Pennsylvania-German Potters"
"Marks of American Potters"
"Salt Glazed Stoneware," "Tin Enameled Pottery"
"Artificial Soft Paste Porcelain"
"Lead Glazed Pottery," Etc.

PRINTED FOR THE MUSEUM
MEMORIAL HALL, FAIRMOUNT PARK
PHILADELPHIA
1908

PREFACE

In entering an entirely new field of research the investigator is hampered at the outset by the entire absence of landmarks, established by his predecessors, from which explorations might be continued into less well-known domains. In the preparation of a monograph on the Maiolica of Mexico the author has had no previously published accounts of this industry to guide him. Starting with only the unverified tradition that pottery, in the style of the earthenware of Talavera, Spain, had been produced somewhere in Mexico at a remote period, it was necessary to follow out each clue that could be discovered, and to unfold the history of the art, step by step. The results of these investigations, extending over several years, are presented in the following pages. While there is yet much to be learned concerning the subject, we now know that soon after the Conquest of Mexico, tin enameled pottery was being produced in that country, although ceramic writers have heretofore believed that its manufacture was never attempted in the Western Hemisphere.

Attention was first called to the existence of stanniferous faience in Mexico in a paper by the present writer, which appeared in the *Bulletin of the Pennsylvania Museum* of July, 1906, which contribution to knowledge was later incorporated in the Museum's Art Primer Number 5, on *Tin Enameled Pottery.* The announcement of this important discovery aroused widespread interest among ceramic students in Europe, as well as in the United States and Mexico. To investigate the subject more fully the author visited the latter country in November, 1907, where an opportunity

3

was presented to study the ware itself and to collect data relating to the history of this little-known art.

Although the wares here treated are more of the nature of the stanniferous faience of Holland, France and Germany than of the maiolica of Italy, and will therefore by some authorities be considered as not entitled to classification with true maiolica, the term has been used here for the reason that the ware is undoubtedly an offshoot of the maiolica of Spain, which reflects the art of the Italian potters. While the enameled ware of Mexico was never lustered like the Italian and Hispano-Moresque, and was not coated with a wash of lead glaze to impart brilliancy, it nevertheless possesses many of the characteristics of both.

The writer takes pleasure in acknowledging his indebtedness to Señor Enrique L. Ventosa, of Puebla, and to Mrs. Zelia Nuttall, of Coyoacán, for valuable assistance in his investigations in Mexico; to Mr. Albert Pepper, and M. Gaston de Ramaix, Secretary of the Belgium Legation, both of the City of Mexico, and to Dr. Wilhelm Bauer, of Tacubaya, for photographs of important examples of Mexican maiolica in private hands; to Rev. Francis S. Borton, of Puebla, for his researches among the early publications of Mexico and the manuscript records of the city of Puebla, through which many of the facts set forth in the following pages have been obtained; and finally to Mr. Albert H. Pitkin, of Hartford, who accompanied the author to Mexico, for invaluable advice and assistance in securing examples of the ware for the Museum collection.

The colored plates have been reproduced from drawings made from the originals by students of the School of Industrial Art connected with this Museum, and by Señor Ventosa, of Puebla.

E. A. B.

Philadelphia, July 30, 1908.

CONTENTS

LIST OF ILLUSTRATIONS

Maiolica Vase, Puebla, about 1800. Colored Plate. Frontispiece.

7

THE MAIOLICA OF MEXICO

I. Tin Enameled Pottery.

The practice of glazing or enameling earthenware with tin, in combination with oxide of lead, is believed to have originated in Babylonia or Assyria centuries ago, and was adopted by the potters of Italy and the Moorish potters of Spain as early as the fourteenth century. The production of maiolica, a variety of tin enameled pottery, in great abundance, in Italy during the fifteenth and sixteenth centuries, resulted in the extension of the manufacture to other parts of Europe, where, under various names, it continued to be made throughout the two centuries following. The Delft wares of Holland and England; the stanniferous faience of France, Belgium, Sweden, Germany, Hungary, and Denmark, were almost identical in body and glaze with the maiolica of Italy and the Hispano-Moresque pottery. Later the Italian influence made itself felt in various parts of Spain,—at Talavera, Alcora, Seville and other places.

For several years past travelers in Mexico have been bringing back to the United States isolated examples of tin enameled pottery, picked up in out-of-the-way places and curiosity shops, and believed to be of Spanish introduction. These occasional pieces escaped the scrutiny of experts and remained unidentified in private collections until the writer's attention was attracted by some examples of what were described as native porcelain, offered for sale by a firm in the city of Mexico, which turned out to be tin enameled pottery. Later several objects of similar character were noticed in the Boston Museum of Fine Arts, in a small collection of pottery which had been gathered together in Mexico

9

by Dr. Denman W. Ross, of Cambridge, Mass. These
pieces, decorated in blue, consisted of small vases, drug
jars and ink-stands, of an entirely different character from
the familiar modern Mexican pottery with which they were
exhibited. The glaze appeared to be stanniferous and the
shapes of the vessels bore no resemblance to those of native
Indian or Mexican production. A brown painted candle-
stick, purchased in Mexico by Mr. Herbert Jaques, of Boston, from an old woman who offered a few articles for sale
in front of one of the churches, presented similar characteristics. No definite information could be obtained regard-
ing the origin of these objects. By some they were called
"Talavera" ware, because they were presumably from the
place of that name in Spain, while others ingeniously
claimed that they were the productions of a noted clay-
worker of the name of Talavera, and at least one Mexican
archæologist entertained the belief that the ware had been
produced in New Spain by Japanese or Chinese potters
brought from the Philippines by the Dominican friars.
These explanations were unconvincing. Then followed a
correspondence, extending over several months, between
the writer and various persons in Mexico, which finally resulted in the interesting discovery that stanniferous faience
had actually been produced in that country, under Spanish
influence, particularly in the city of Puebla, where at a
remote period numerous maiolica factories had flourished.
Further investigation resulted in the acquisition of several
characteristic pieces of the ware for the Museum, which
served as a nucleus around which the present remarkable
collection, which forms the basis for the preparation of this
monograph, has been gathered.

II. Industrial Activity of the Spaniards in Mexico.

Immediately after the conquest of Mexico, in 1520, Spain began to graft her civilization on the ruder civilization of the New World. The flower of her clergy, soldiery and artisans poured into the new El Dorado, where they at once established the printing press and introduced the industrial methods of the Old World. Factories for the manufacture of staple goods were erected at many places. The natives of Mexico, already skilful craftsmen, soon came to excel their teachers in proficiency, and in a few years New Spain had become independent of Europe in the various industrial arts. During the eighty years, between the date of the Conquest and the close of the sixteenth century, greater progress was made in Mexico in literature, architecture, and the other useful arts, than in any other country on the Western Continent in a similar period.

In 1580 "the manufactories of Puebla and Oaxaca were able to produce a good quantity of silk goods manufactured from the raw materials sent them from Asiatic markets. The cloth manufactories in 1580 consumed 12,000 arrobas (300,000 pounds) of wool, grown in the colony. In 1582, according to Señor J. G. Icazbalceta, there were manufactured in Mexico 9000 dozens of *naipes* (playing cards), a sad indication of the tastes of the people. These cards were held in higher esteem than those brought from Spain."*

Referring to the natural abilities of the Mexicans, Men-

---

* Vide *Mexico y Su Evolucion Social,* by Don Justo Sierra. Mexico, 1901. Vol. II, p. 125.

dieta, writing in 1580-1596, states* that "after they became Christians and saw our images from Flanders and Italy, there is no altar ornament or image, however beautiful it may be, that they will not reproduce and imitate. There were artisans in *pottery* and *clay vessels* for eating and drinking purposes, and these were very well made and colored, although the workmen *did not know how to glaze them. But they soon learned that from the first craftsman who came over from Spain, in spite of all he could do to guard and hide the secret from them.* . . . And finally this may be understood as a general rule,—that nearly all the beautiful and curious works of every class of trades and arts that are now (1596) being carried forward in the Indies (at least in New Spain, or Mexico) are being done and finished by the Indians; because the Spanish masters of all these trades, wonderful to state, do nothing more than charge the Indians with the work, telling them how they wish it done, and the Indians proceed to do it in so perfect a manner that it could not be bettered."

Juan de Torquemada† quotes from a royal decree, in 1614, in regard to the enforced labor of Indians in the factories of Mexico: "In this case I grant you discretionary power and authority to allow that (the Indians) may serve and hire themselves only in those factories already established at the time of the date of this decree in the cities and suburbs of Mexico, Puebla and Mechuacan, but under the following limitations." This decree is signed Yo El Rey (I, myself, the King), May 6, 1609.

H. H. Bancroft, the historian, states that "Long be-

---

* *Historia Eclesiastica Indiana obra escrita a fines del siglo XVI*, por Fray Geronimo de Mendieta. La publica por primera Vez Joaquin Garcia Icazbalceta, Mexico, 1870, p. 404.

† *Monarquia Indiana*. Por Juan de Torquemada. Sevilla, 1614, pp. 308-9.

fore the conquest the Indians had been experts in the manufacture of earthenware and pottery. Under Spanish rule (1531-1800) the variety of design was greatly increased and a larger field was opened to them. They also learned the fabrication of glass, and as this industry gradually developed, several factories arose, chiefly at Puebla, where forty-six establishments for the making of glass and pottery were in a flourishing condition in 1793. Subsequently a decline took place, and in the beginning of this century the number was reduced to eighteen."*

It is stated by Luis Moreri that in 1753 Puebla was of importance, "due to her cloth manufactories, as good as those of Spain, as well as those of hats, money and glassware."†

Don Lucas Alaman‡ tells us that in the year 1803 there were exported from the port of Vera Cruz to various points in America 700 cases of pottery from Puebla.

---

* *History of Mexico.* Six vols. 1890. Vol. III, p. 620.

† *El Gran Diccionario Historico, ó Miscelánea Curiosa de la Historia Sagrada y Profana,* etc. Paris, 1753. Ten vols. fol. Tomo I, p. 519.

‡ *Historia de Mejico.* Mexico, 1849-52.

III. Puebla, the Centre of Maiolica Manufacture in Mexico.

The city of Puebla, or La Puebla de los Angeles (the Town of the Angels), as it was formerly called, situated about one hundred and eighty-six kilometers southwest of the City of Mexico by rail, was founded as a new city by the Spaniards in 1531 or 1532. Here were established some of the first manufactories by European craftsmen in the New World. Among these were numerous glass factories and potteries, and it is a curious fact that for nearly three centuries this city continued to be the only centre, so far as we know, of the maiolica industry in the Western Hemisphere.

The following translation of the story of the founding of the city of Puebla is given by Thomas A. Janvier, in his *Mexican Guide**:

†"Passing by the tradition that in ancient times, before the blessed light of Christianity ever shone in these parts, the unregenerate heathen saw visions of angels marshalled in mighty hosts in the heavens above where the city now stands, let us come at once to a stable groundwork of ascertained fact. In the year of our Lord 1529 came to Tlaxcala the illustrious Fray Julian Garces, the first consecrated bishop of the Catholic Church whose feet, shod with Pontifical holiness, ever trod in this heathen Edom. Even before his coming the project had been mooted of

---

* Charles Scribner's Sons, New York, 1890, p. 389.

† *Puebla Sagrada y Profana. Informe dado a su muy ilustre Ayuntamiento el Año de 1746.* Por el M. R. P. Fray Juan Villa Sanchez, religioso del convento de Santo Domingo.

14

founding somewhere in these parts a town that might be a resting-place in the long and weary walk from the coast to the City of Mexico. With this project the new Bishop was in hearty accord; yet was he uncertain in his mind as to where best might be placed the new town.

"As all know, it ofttimes happens that one dreams in the night of those things of which one thinks most by day. Thus it was that one night this venerable gentleman, being retired to the humble bed upon which he took his scanty rest, dreamed a prophetic dream. In his vision, while his spirit was controlled by a superior power, he beheld a most beautiful plain (*hermosisima vega*) bounded by the great slope of the volcanoes westward, broken by two little hills a league asunder, dotted by many springs, and cut by two rivers which gave abundant water and made all things fresh and green. And as he gazed, in pleased amazement, at this charming place, lo! he saw two angels who with line and rod measured bounds and distances upon the ground— as do those who plan the founding of great buildings and mark where shall be wide streets and open squares. And having beheld this vision, the Bishop awoke.

"Straightway he set himself, that very hour, to searching for the site that, as his vision had shown him, was chosen of the angels. And as he walked, being, no doubt, divinely ordered in his goings, he came to the very plain that he had seen in his dream. Then gladly he exclaimed: 'This is the site that the Lord has chosen through his holy angels; and here, to His glory, shall the city be!'" And on this spot, at the feet of the great mountains, Popocatepetl and Ixtaccihuatl, was built La Puebla de los Angeles, which during the three and three-quarters centuries of its existence, has grown to be a city of some 98,000 inhabitants, and one of the foremost manufacturing centres in the present Republic of Mexico.

At the beginning of the seventeenth century, according to Juan N. Del Valle,* "Puebla was already a beautiful city, in which were reunited all material beauties which can be produced by the combination of wealth and good taste. On the other hand the native talent of her sons for the useful arts was revealed each day more and more, in excellent weaves of wool and cotton, in pottery and glassware and in many other handicrafts which in those times might well sustain a comparison with the products of Europe. . . . The pottery of Puebla has been so perfected that with satisfaction we have seen pieces that rivaled foreign pottery, in form as well as in design."

Thomas Gage, who was in Puebla in 1625, writing in 1648†, says concerning its manufactures at that time: "This City of the Angels is now thought to consist of ten thousand inhabitants. That which maketh it most famous is the Cloth which is made in it, and is sent far and near, and judged now to be as good as the Cloth of Segovia, which is the best that is made in Spain, but now is not so much esteemed of, nor sent so much from Spain to America, by reason of the abundance of fine Cloth which is made in this City of the Angels. The felts likewise that are made are the best of all that country. There is likewise a Glass house, which is there a rarity, none other being as yet known in those parts. But the Mint-house that is in it, where is coyned half the Silver that cometh from Sacatecas, makes it second to Mexico; and it is thought that in time it will be as great and populous as Mexico."

Reverendo Padre Fray Augustin de Vetancurt states (*Tratado de la Ciudad de la Puebla*, page 47)‡ that "In the

---

* *Guia de Forasteros de la Capital de Puebla para el año de 1842.*
† *A New Survey of the Indies.* London, 1648.
‡ *Teatro Mexicano Descripcion Breve de los Sucessos Exemplares Historicos, Politicos, Militares, y Religiosos del Nuevo Mundo Occidental de las Indias.* Mexico, 1698.

city of Puebla are to be found all the industries which go to make up a Republic, and in *glazed earthenware,* glassware, cutlery and soap, they surpass all the rest in New Spain. The glazed pottery is finer than that of Talabera, and can compete with that of China in its fineness. The glassware, although not so fine, is like that of Venice. The temper of their knives and scissors exceeds that of all others, like the blades of Toledo." This shows that glazed pottery was being made in Puebla previous to 1690, since the first "Licencia" in the book is dated Madrid, April 17, 1692, at which time the industry had already reached a high state of excellence.

The same writer remarks that "there were (among the Indians) artisans who made pots and large and small jars of clay and crocks, painted and very ornamental. *But they did not learn how to glaze their wares until the Spaniards showed them,* and now they make clay pottery of various and pleasing designs."*

Fray Juan Villa Sanchez,† writing in 1745, states that "Glassware forms part of the commerce of Puebla, which is not equaled in any other part of the kingdom. If it does not compete with that of Venice it at least equals that of France; thick, smooth, clean and very clear, and it is made in pieces of exquisite workmanship. The pottery, of which great quantities are made in Puebla, is similar to the glassware, being so fine and beautiful that it equals or excels that of Talavera, or of Cartagena of the Indies, the ambition of the Puebla potters being to emulate and equal the beauty of the wares of China. There is a great demand for this product, especially for the most ordinary qualities, which are most in demand throughout the kingdom."

---

* Ibid. Vol. I, p. 60.
† *Puebla Sagrada y Profana.* Puebla, 1746.

IV. A Potters' Guild in Puebla.

No previous writer, so far as we are aware, has made any reference to the existence of trade guilds in Mexico during the seventeenth century. The remarkable development of certain industries in Puebla within a century or so after the conquest of the country by Spain would naturally lead us to suppose that some sort of organization for the mutual protection and aid of craftsmen in various branches of art should have been attempted, since we know that guilds have existed in Europe from the seventh century. It was believed that if any record of such associations should have been preserved it would probably be found among the archives of the city. The Rev. Francis S. Borton, a student of Mexican bibliography, was employed by this Museum to search the official manuscripts, which, after obtaining the necessary permission from the Ayuntamiento, or Council of the city, he proceeded to do. The results of his investigations proved to be even more gratifying than had been expected. It was found that a potters' guild had in reality existed in Puebla between the years 1653 and 1676, and that a code of laws for the regulation of the manufacture and sale of pottery had been enacted. Dr. Borton has transcribed and translated these ancient laws, which, since they throw much light on the history of the art, we give here in full.

EXTRACTS FROM THE LAWS FOR THE TRADE GUILDS. FOLIO, VELLUM BINDING, MS. 1653-1676. ARCHIVES OF THE CITY OF LA PUEBLA DE LOS ANGELES (LAWS FOR THE POTTERS).

1st. No person may practice the trade of a potter without being examined in that trade by the Alcaldes and Inspectors, which officials shall be nominated and elected to their office by the master workmen of the guild.

To that end each year their names shall be put down and their election shall be verified before a notary. And this election shall be in the presence of a Justice and shall be sworn to. And the Justice shall give the Alcaldes and Inspectors-elect power to visit the stores and work-shops, and to condemn the work which is found not to be in accord with the tenor of the following articles.

2d. That taking into consideration the fact that to-day there is not a single master workman (of the potters' guild) who has passed an examination and that until the present there have never been any laws for the examination and government of potters: therefore we have been nominated for that position; we are to be the examiners. By virtue of our nominations as experts in pottery making we have been approved and are examiners according to the law.

3d. No negro, mulatto, nor person of mixed blood can be allowed to take the examination for a master potter. The provisions of this article must be strictly complied with.

4th. That in order to justify the existing laws no persons who have not been examined (as mentioned) shall work at the potter's trade, or possess pottery-stores or potteries.

Such persons there may be who pretend to have these rights for a limited time, and that they were exempt from the examination. All which is greatly against the interests of all real master potters. No Judge shall grant such a license to any person whatsoever, nor shall the Alcaldes or Inspectors either tacitly or expressly permit such persons (unexamined) to have potteries, under whatsoever pretext or excuse or palliation.

5th. There shall be known three classes of pottery, the fine, the common and the yellow, such as jars, pots, vases, pans, strainers, etc. No one can manufacture pottery, either fine or common, without passing the examination required in the kind of pottery he expects to make. He may only make the kind in whose manufacture he is examined, unless perchance his examination has been on all (three kinds).

6th. The widow of a master potter may continue his plant and shop, and none may interfere with her right; and the son of a master potter can continue the business of his deceased father for three years without being examined, but at the end of that time he must be examined.

7th. All master potters who have been examined shall familiarize themselves with these laws, so that they shall be able to comply with them, and not plead ignorance.

8th. For the making of said pottery the following rules are to be observed.

1. First the clay from which the various kinds of pottery are to be made must be well sifted and cleaned, in order that it may obtain the proper baking and perfection necessary for its durability.

2. The glaze for the fine pottery must be properly mixed and treated; to one arroba (25 lbs.) of lead add six pounds of tin, and these must be well mixed and baked. If the ware is to be painted, it must first be decorated with black, in order that its beauty may shine out, and each piece must be of an equal thickness in its parts.

3. All the common and white pottery shall have a glaze made of one arroba of lead, and two pounds of tin well mingled and carefully prepared. In this common pottery are to be included white, medium, and painted, in all sorts of vessels.

4. The glazing should correspond with the different wares, and should also be well ground, very liquid and without impurities, so that the ware of whatever class may be durable and honestly made.

5. Ordinary plates for the table should have a fourth of border, in fine ware as well as in the common, and these plates should not exceed in thickness the edge of a real, and there should be an equal thickness in all parts: because in this combination results less facility in breaking and chipping and more facility in boxing and shipping. For, otherwise, well known bad results follow. This degree and union of qualities (above mentioned) should be understood as applying to all classes of pottery generally.

6. All ordinary bowls (cups (?))* should be from edge to edge an eighth (of a vara:†—4⅛ inches). In the finer pottery other dimensions may be used, such as are to the taste of potter and purchaser. Of course one knows that the coarse ware will not answer the purposes of the finer.

7. In order to avoid all the perplexities that might otherwise occur, each master potter shall have a clearly marked stamp or monogram (for the wares made by him), and on all pottery made by him this stamp or trade-mark must appear. Said mark shall be placed on the examination paper of each master potter, so that he may not deny being the maker of any and all pottery bearing that stamp.

All Alcaldes and Inspectors shall take particular precaution with regard to these private trade-marks that they give out, and not duplicate them.

And to avoid that, they should have a book in which shall be entered the name of each master potter examined by them, and a facsimile of the particular stamp or trade-mark issued to him.

And this book shall be passed on successively to the different Alcaldes and Inspectors, as they are elected year by year.

---

* The word *escudilla,* in the original, means porringer.
† A *vara* is 33 inches.

8. Whoever shall countermark or falsify the trade-mark of another shall incur the penalties provided for all such cases, and shall suffer both in his person and in his goods.

9. For the annoyances arising from the practice just mentioned prejudice very seriously the interests not only of the community but of the master potters also; because under pretext of helping the falsifying potters there are persons who, seeing their necessity, sell them the prime materials at increased prices, and then allow the said potters to pay them in pottery.

Thus these persons go about gathering up and monopolizing large quantities of this inferior pottery, and afterward sell it at exorbitant prices.

And as this spurious ware is neither finished nor baked as it should be, the speculators carry it to different parts where they sell it or trade it for merchandise.

And those who buy it find themselves deceived, and from this results injury to the purchasers and discredit to the legitimate master potters.

So it is prohibited to all persons to buy said pottery with the object of re-selling it under whatever pretext. Only the master potters can sell it in their houses, or in public shops, and the market places,—but not in the streets, to avoid the robberies to which the master potters are there subject.

The penalty for transgressing this law shall be a fine of twenty dollars, of which one-fourth shall go to the Exchequer, one-fourth to the Denouncer, one-fourth to the Judge, and one-fourth to the expenses and conservation of the potters' guild.

The above is the penalty for the first infringement; for the second offence the fine shall be doubled, and for the third offence the culprit shall be left to the discretion of the Judge.

10. When an apprentice shall have finished the time during which his master was obligated to instruct him, he shall go before the Alcaldes and the Inspectors to show what he has learned; and if he be found deficient, according to the declaration of said Inspectors who have examined him, then he shall go to the Justice to implore that his teacher be compelled to finish his instruction at his (the master's) expense.

In the manner set forth we have made and do make laws for all the faithful of our potters' guild, that they may govern themselves thereby; and we protest that whenever time and experience shall demonstrate that it would be for the advantage of the guild to add other sections to these set forth, it may be done.

And we swear by God and the Cross that these laws have been framed without any fraud or any ulterior motives.

And we herewith sign our names, with the exception of Andres de Haro who does not know how to write.

Done in the City of Los Angeles of New Spain, May 10, 1653.

Diego Salvador Carreto
Damian Hernandez

Continueth:

And Señor the Duke of Albuquerque governing this New Spain, approved and confirmed said laws, sending his mandate on June 30, 1659.

And now Juan Felix Galvez (in the name of Diego Salvador Carreto, a master potter, and in the name of the other master potters, and the Potters' Guild, citizens of the City of Los Angeles), represented to me (the undersigned), that in order that said laws, herewithin inserted, might be guarded and observed,—he begged me to be pleased to order that said laws should be cried in said City of the Angels, and that they should be copied in the books of the Corporation of that city.

Of which I ordered notice to be given to the Attorney General, Señor Dr. Don Manuel Escalante y Mendoza, Knight of the Order of St. James, who gave the following reply:—

Most Excellent Sir:—

His Majesty's Attorney General says that by permission of your Excellency, he will concede to the Petitioner the insertion of the mandate among the laws, which is what he asks.

Mexico, March 23, 1662. Don Manuel de Escalante y Mendoza.

Upon which the correspondence was all sent by Licentiate Don Alonso de Alvarez Pinelo, Advocate of the Royal Audience, to the Assessor General, in order that he might, as he afterward did, give his opinion in the case, which was as follows:—

Opinion:—

Most Excellent Señor:—

May it please you to order that the wishes of the petitioners be granted, in accordance with the ruling of the Attorney General.

Mexico, March 26, 1662.

Licentiate Don Alonso de Alvarez.

As for the rest of the matter, in conformity with the above expressed Opinion (of the Assessor) for the present, I approve and confirm these laws herein inserted, and order the Justices, the Corporation and the Aldermen of the City of Los Angeles, that they procure that said laws be guarded, and kept and executed in all and their several parts, both in their letter and spirit; and that said authorities shall have said laws written in the book of ordinances, and in the books of the deputation, in order that there may be knowledge (of said laws) forever, and I also order that said laws shall be cried publicly in the usual places in the city, that said laws may be observed, and that to the crier be delivered the original of this mandate.

Mexico, March 28, 1662.
The Marquis Count of Vaños,
By order of his Excellency
Don Pedro Velasquez de la Cadena.

Petition:—

Antonio Marques of Santillana (Spain), Roque of Talavera (Spain), and José Ramos,—master potters all in the business of a potter in white ware, residents in this city of Los Angeles, appear before your worships and set forth the following:—

That in order to know and understand what we should do in our art and trade—it would be a very great favor to our Potters' Guild if the present most excellent and honorable Corporation would hand over to us the originals of those laws that relate to our trade and office, and stating what are all our rights, privileges and obligations. Of course in the hands of the Corporation would remain all necessary public and attested evidence that the original laws had been entrusted to us of the Potters' Guild.

For which we beg and entreat your worships that you be pleased to order that said laws relating to potters be given to us, and that the public notary here make a note of the same in due and proper form, and that said laws be publicly cried, according to the mandate given by the Supreme Government of this New Spain. And may it be included in said laws, that justice be done to all concerned,—which is what we ask.

And now we put an end to this writing, according to all necessary forms, etc., etc.

Antonio Marques of Santillana, Spain.

Roque of Talavera, Spain.

Antonio de Galvez, Solicitor.

Public Notice:—

In the City of Los Angeles on August 22 of 1676, being met in the gateway of the ordinary common court, with a great concourse of people assisting,—after a trumpet had been sounded,—by the voice of Juan Flores the public crier, in loud and clear tones was cried the mandate, set forth on the sheets preceding this, on the part of the most excellent Señor Marquis Count of Bolaños, who was formerly Viceroy of this New Spain,—in which public crying were also included the laws for potters in fine, common and yellow ware.

And witnesses of this act were Don Francisco Solano, one of his Majesty's notaries; Diego de Aviña, and José del Castillo, these being present in person, together with many other people.

All of which I certify to be true.

The Notary.

In my presence:—

Miguel Zenon Zapata, Notary for the Crown and for the Corporation.

A few explanations.

1st. The common pottery. Plates and cups painted in poor blue; the porcelains and large plates painted in the manner that we call "aborronado" (blurred, blotted); and this should be in blue and two other colors; and then the common white ware with a stamp or maker's trade-mark only that it may be recognized, as in the case of all classes of ware.

2d. The fine pottery. In the fine ware the *armados* (groundwork (?)) should be painted in blue and finished in black with dots along the borders and edges of all ware painted in this style.

And in order that there may be variety, the other style of decoration for this fine ware *shall be in imitation of the Talavera ware,* or figures and designs in colors, shading them with all the five colors used in the art. The manufacture of this fine ware shall be with the greatest neatness and cleanliness possible. Each piece should be baked in its own *pedaño* or *casuela*,* and the kiln should be charged the same, and the baking should be the same as for the common ware. For the merit of the fine ware consists in the superior cleanliness of its preparation, and finish. But fine ware must not be baked, not a piece of it, with *caballitos*† ("little horses") nor *sicoles*;† only in the baking of ordinary ware was such an inartistic process thought of and permitted.

3d. Also in making the fine wares the coloring should be *in imitation of the Chinese ware,* very blue, finished in the same style and with *relief work in blue,* and on this style of pottery there should be painted black dots and grounds in colors.

From the foregoing laws regulating the pottery industry in Puebla, taken from the archives of that city, we learn that in the year 1653 the manufacture of maiolica in Mexico had already reached such a stage of importance that

---

* Seggars.

† Clay supports used under and around the cheap wares in stacking them in the kiln.

it was deemed necessary to formulate rules for the protection of the potters themselves and the maintenance of the
standard of their wares. The statement that at that time
there was not a single master workman of the guild who
had passed an examination and that there had never been
any laws providing for the examination and government of
potters clearly indicates that the pottery industry had
flourished in Puebla for some time previous. We may therefore believe that the art of maiolica manufacture had been
established in New Spain at least as early as the end of
the sixteenth century.

The first examiners of the guild were Diego Salvador
Carreto, Damian Hernandez and Andres de Haro. The
rules they formulated were intended to regulate the quality
of the various grades of ware, the sizes of plates, bowls, etc.,
and provided for the stamping of individual marks on the
ware, by which the products of different potters should be
known. The penalties for transgressing these laws were
clearly set forth.

A few years later (apparently in 1662) Antonio Marques, of Santillana, Spain, Roque of Talavera, Spain, and
José Ramos, master potters of Puebla, representing the
guild, petitioned the city to turn over to the guild the
originals of the laws relating to the trade, setting forth
the rights, privileges and obligations of potters. The petitioners, it will be noted, were Spanish potters from Santillana and Talavera, who, having learned their trade in Spain,
had become leading members of the craft in Mexico. It is
reasonable to suppose that the methods employed in Spain
would be continued by these workmen in their new field of
labor and in support of this supposition we find in the de-
scription of the various wares specified in the laws of the
guild that one style of decoration for the finest ware was
to be in imitation of the Talavera ware, the designs of which

were to be in colors shaded with all the five colors used in the art.

At this early date we find that the influence of the Chinese potters had already made itself felt, for it was also specified that, in order to give variety to the best wares, the coloring should also be "in imitation of the Chinese ware, very blue, finished in the same style and with relief work in blue." This reference to Chinese ware shows that Oriental porcelain must have been imported in considerable quantities into Mexico previous to 1653, fully a century before trade relations of any importance were established between China and the American Colonies, now the United States of America, for while it is true that in New England a limited amount of imported table ware was owned by wealthy people, as early as the middle of the seventeenth century, we have no evidence that decorative pieces, such as vases, found their way into the British Colonies to the north of Mexico until well into the eighteenth century.

These manuscript laws for the guild throw much light on the nature of the wares produced in the latter half of the seventeenth century in Mexico. The clay was to be most carefully prepared. The composition of the glaze was definitely prescribed,—six pounds of tin to twenty-five pounds of lead for the fine ware, and for the common pottery two parts of tin to twenty-five parts of lead. The groundwork of one variety of fine ware was to be painted in blue finished in black with dots along the borders and edges, and in imitating Chinese porcelains the decorations were to be painted with black dots and colored grounds.

We are somewhat at a loss to explain the meaning of the instructions which required the groundwork of certain fine ware to be painted in blue. We have not met with a single example so treated. The early maiolica vases do not appear to have ever been painted with a solid dark blue ground, although in some there are borders and panels, or medallions, with reserved designs in white in a blue ground. The nearest approach to this style of work is shown in the vase illustrated in the text cut, No. 18. Some of the early tiles were also treated in like manner (see illustration 39). Among the best examples of this character are the tiles of the old church of San Miguel, Puebla, in which the reserved figures are colored yellow and orange (see illustration 55). But even in these somewhat rare examples the ground is irregular and mottled, according to the uneven application and varying depth of the blue enamel. It is true that one variety of ware was covered with an even, thin ground of pale, grayish blue, but such pieces were not produced until the nineteenth century and belong to the period of decadence.

We are even more puzzled to understand what was meant by finishing the designs with black dots along borders and edges. Not a single piece so treated seems to have come to light, and we can only conclude that this rule was not literally observed by the potters. Many pieces, however, are found in which the outlines are accentuated by the use of blue dots, particularly those in the Chinese style.

The most important law was that concerning trademarks. Each master potter was required to use a clearly marked stamp or monogram on all pieces of ware made by him and this individual mark was to be attached to his examination paper. Inspectors were charged to exercise the greatest precaution against duplicating these distinguishing marks, which were to be recorded in a book with the names of the potters to whom they had been issued.

How long these laws were in force we have no means of ascertaining, but it is apparent that they were in operation at least throughout the third quarter of the seventeenth century. During that period, it is to be presumed, all products of the Puebla potteries were marked with some distinguishing device. Such pieces are now rare, but several examples bearing the initials or monograms of the makers, painted in blue, may be seen in the Museum collection (see chapter on Marks).

V. Pueblan Potters.

As we have already seen, the pottery industry was of sufficient importance in Puebla in 1653, to require the passage of laws for the government of potters, but there appear to be no records which throw light on the extent of the manufacture of maiolica or the number of craftsmen engaged therein. From the laws for the potters we learn that in the year above mentioned Diego Salvador Carreto, Damian Hernandez and Andres de Haro were prominent members of the craft, and that in 1662 Antonio Marques, of Santillana, Spain, one Roque of Talavera, Spain, and José Ramos were master potters in Puebla. It is not probable that these were the first clay workers sent from Spain, as evidence is not lacking that the fictile art had been practiced in Mexico by Europeans for fully fifty years before the establishment of the guild. In addition to the Spanish potters there were numerous native workers in clay, some of whom learned the art of glazing and became proficient maiolists.

Señor Enrique L. Ventosa, who has given much attention to the subject, states, as a result of his historical investigations, based on tradition and information obtained from some of the older potters whose ancestors for several generations produced tin enameled pottery in Puebla, that towards the middle of the seventeenth century there were ten or twelve maiolica manufacturers in that city. About a hundred years later (1750), when the industry had reached its height, some thirty establishments were in operation, but from about 1800 to 1860 the number had decreased to about twelve. At the present time, only six manufactories of tin enameled earthenware are in operation in Puebla, where the common grade of utilitarian wares, and tiles, entirely devoid of artistic merit, are manufactured. The proprietors of these *locerias* are as follows: Dimas Uriarte, Luis Guevara, Ignacio Romero, Hilario Romero, J. M. Sanchez and Antonio Espinosa. At the latter's establishment Señor Ventosa is engaged in decorating the most artistic ware which is now being made in Mexico, having since 1900 been endeavoring to elevate the standard of an art, which, after having flourished for over two hundred years, has fallen into decay. This artist has recently been reviving many of the designs found on the old maiolica and tiles of Spain and Mexico. His work is characterized by conscientious adherence to the spirit of the originals, and some of his large plaques, in Hispano-Moresque style, are especially praiseworthy. Señor Ventosa's reproductions are sold at moderate prices, and are so characteristic in treatment that they can be distinguished without difficulty from the older pieces which served as his models (see illustration 59).

Señor Ventosa, who came from Barcelona, Spain, having pursued his art education in Paris, commenced in 1900 to reproduce the antique wares of Puebla. So successful was he in this work that all of the other tin enamel factories of that city have followed his lead and at present are engaged in imitating, to a greater or lesser extent, the older forms, in addition to the legitimate manufacture of commercial products. Some of the larger pieces occasionally find their way into the hands of dealers and collectors where they pose as veritable antiques, readily deceiving all but the closest student of the ancient wares. A pair of enormous vases, in Chinese style, mounted with dome-shaped covers, and embellished with figure paintings illustrating scenes relating to the Conquest of Mexico, were recently brought to the attention of the writer as examples of seventeenth century work. Investigation proved them to have been produced within a year or so, at one of the establishments which are still in existence (see illustration 60).

VI. Processes of Manufacture.

The present day potters of Puebla, Mexico, use practically the same processes as were employed by the European maiolists of the seventeenth and eighteenth centuries, since there has been little change in methods in this industry for hundreds of years.

When the clay has been well mixed by the feet of the workmen, and freed from grit, it is fashioned into vessels, which are laid aside to dry, and afterwards placed in the first kiln and subjected to heat for five or six hours, being taken out in the biscuit state. The baked ware is then dipped in a liquid preparation of glaze or enamel, composed of oxides of lead and tin, ground together in the proportion of about three parts of the former to one of the latter, to which water, sand and a little molasses have been added, the latter to make it adhesive. After the glaze has dried on the surface of the porous clay, the decorations are painted in colors obtained from metallic oxides mixed with flux. When perfectly dry the ware is subjected to a second firing, which lasts about thirty-six hours. By this process the colors are incorporated with the glaze, presenting the appearance of underglaze painting.

The Mexican maiolica differs from the Italian in that the former does not possess a superficial coating of glaze, composed of oxide of lead, potash and sand, as in the latter, known as *marzacotto*, the lead being mixed into the enamel before it is applied, by the Mexican potters. For this reason the Mexican ware possesses a homogeneous enamel, which is so hard that it can only with difficulty be scratched with a steel point.

A careful study of the body of Puebla maiolica reveals the fact that the clays employed were apparently of two kinds, white and red. These two varieties will be found to occur in the earliest pieces as well as those of recent date. The white body is much softer than the red, the difference in color being caused by the degree of heat to which the ware was subjected at the first firing, or the length of time it was allowed to remain in the kiln. When baked slightly the clay appears white and porous, and so soft that it can be readily cut with a knife, but when allowed to remain longer in the kiln, at a high temperature, it becomes partially vitrified and considerably harder, and of a deep pink or reddish hue, increasing in density with the darkening of the color. Thus the tint of the body bears no relation to the antiquity of the ware nor does it indicate the locality from which the clay was obtained.* It is true that two varieties of clay are used,—white clay obtained at San Bartolo, San Pedro and Santo Tomas, hills near the village of Totomehuacán, five kilometers from Puebla, and red clay from Loreto and Guadalupe, in the vicinity of that city, but these are always combined in equal parts, to produce the results desired. It is stated that no other combination of clays is employed and that neither the red nor the white clay can be used alone, with satisfactory results.

It will be noticed that in the rules of the potters' guild of the seventeenth century it is stated that the glaze for fine pottery shall consist of twenty-five pounds of lead to six pounds of tin, or four and one-sixth parts of the former

---

* It is a curious fact, however, that many of the best pieces of the earlier ware were only slightly fired and, as a result, possess a light-colored body, which in some instances is almost as soft as chalk, but is always covered with a hard enamel. The larger and coarser pieces were usually burned more thoroughly and are consequently more vitreous and of a darker tint beneath the glaze.

to one of the latter, a somewhat less proportion of tin than is used by the modern potters. In consequence of the greater care exercised in the preparation of materials, however, the glaze of the older ware is more even and homogeneous than that of the present day wares.

Each piece was baked in its own fire-clay case, or seggar, and the use of clay supports, which would leave scars on the pieces, was prohibited by the laws of the guild for the finer wares.

For the common wares, among which were probably included tiles, the glaze consisted of a less proportion of tin (twelve and a half parts of lead to one of tin). In baking this grade of ware clay supports were used in stacking the pieces in the kiln instead of enclosing them in seggars, and the scars produced by this practice are distinctly visible on many of the tiles.

Five colors were employed in decorating the best pieces, while three colors were used in the ornamentation of cheaper ware. It is not to be supposed that the employment of so many colors was obligatory, but merely permissible. In point of fact we fail to find, among the earliest pieces of maiolica which have descended to us, any which were painted in polychrome. If five colors were applied before the beginning of the eighteenth century to vases and other ornamental objects, such pieces have apparently disappeared, but on many of the oldest tiles, found in the walls of ancient churches, convents and monasteries, the decorations are frequently in blue, green and yellow. Tiles which had been set in cement where they would remain undisturbed for centuries, would naturally outlast the more perishable objects for household use and decoration.

It was provided in the rules for making pottery that painted ware was to be first decorated with black, "in order that its beauty may shine out." We do not understand from this statement that the ground was to be covered with black nor that the designs should be painted in silhouette, but that the patterns should be *outlined* with black or dark brown and afterwards filled in or shaded with blue or some other color. Many of the earlier pieces which have been preserved were actually so treated, the darker outlines bringing out the designs with greater distinctness on the white enamel of the ground. This is true particularly of many articles which were decorated in the Chinese style.

VII. The Maiolica of Spain.

There were three great centres of maiolica manufacture in Spain, namely, Malaga, Valencia and Talavera. The so-called Hispano-Moresque pottery, or lustered faience, is now ascribed to Malaga and Valencia, having probably been made at a little earlier date at the first mentioned place. The principal features of the Malaga maiolica are golden and pearly lustres combined with dark blue decorations in conventionalized animal and plant forms. The celebrated Alhambra vase, believed by some to date from about the middle of the fourteenth century, is attributed by the best authorities to Malaga.

During the fifteenth and sixteenth centuries Valencia was one of the most important seats of maiolica manufacture in Spain. The chief characteristics are mock Arabic inscriptions and renderings of animal and plant forms, such as vine leaves, briony foilage, animals and birds. Much of the ware is of a heraldic character. Under the name of Valencia ware was that produced in the neighboring towns of Manises, Gesarte, Mislata and Paterna. While the lustered wares of Malaga and Valencia are quite similar in many respects, they can be distinguished from each other in a general way by the character of the decoration, that of the former being distinguished by large, bold motifs, while that of Valencia more frequently consists of smaller and more closely crowded details (see illustration 1).

The tin enameled ware of Talavera de la Reyna, in the Province of Toledo, presents well marked characteristics which are not found in the Hispano-Moresque lustered pottery. Brongniart regards Talavera as the true centre of the manufacture of pottery in Spain. Albert Jacquemart, in his *"Histoire de la Céramique,"* states that this locality was so renowned for its faience in the seventeenth and eighteenth centuries that the name "Talavera" came to be com-

1. HISPANO—MORESQUE MAIOLICA.
PLAQUE AND DRUG JAR, OR ALBARELLO.
Blue and Gold Lustre Decoration.
Sixteenth Century.
In the Boston Museum of Fine Arts.

monly applied to pottery in Spain, just as the word "Delft" was used in a generic sense in Holland and England to indicate all pottery possessing a stanniferous enamel made in those countries. In illustration 2 is shown a Talavera plate, decorated in dark blue, of the early eighteenth century.

Señor Juan F. Riaño, in the South Kensington Handbook on *Spanish Arts*, states that "the earliest mention we find of Talavera pottery occurs in a MS. volume dated 1560 —a history of this town, in which mention is made of 'white, green, blue and other colored Talavera ware.' . . . In a MS. history of Talavera written in 1651 (Bib. Nac. Madrid, G. 112), the author, Father de Ajofrin, says that 'the

2. MAIOLICA PLATE.
Decorated in Blue.
Talavera, Spain, Early Eighteenth Century.
In the Museum Collection.

pottery is as good as that of Pisa, a large number of *azulejos* are also made to adorn the front of altars, churches, gardens, alcoves, saloons, and bowers.' . . . In another MS. history of Talavera (Bibl. Nac. G. 187) we find mention of 'perfect imitations of oriental china' and that the pottery made there, 'was used all over Spain, and sent to India, France, Flanders, Italy and other countries, and was esteemed everywhere for the perfection of the colouring and brilliancy of the glaze.' "

The same writer, quoting from Larruga's "Memories Politicas y Economicas" (vol. X., Madrid, 1741), informs us that "the manufactory of fine earthenware of Talavera de la Reyna continued to make such pottery of importance until 1720; eight kilns existed then, which employed more than 400 persons, men, women and children."

The industry was revived later on, and Udal ap Rhys, in "An Account of the Most Remarkable Places and Curiosities in Spain and Portugal" (London, 1749), referring to Talavera, says, "It is noted also for a very curious kind of earthenware that is made in imitation of China."

In another MS. history of Talavera (Bib. Nac. F. 142), written about 1568, Fr. Andres de Torrejon tells us that "the varnish used for the white pottery is made with tin and sand."

Very little seems to have been published in reference to the exact nature of the maiolica wares of Talavera de la Reyna, but Jacquemart, in his "History of the Ceramic Art,"* describes several pieces of the ware.

Quoting from Jacquemart, "The enamel of Talavera is white and well glazed; from this manufactory have been sent pieces very remarkable in form and decoration; we have seen a large state vase with twisted handles, and opening decorated with a twist in relief; upon the ovoid body twisted mouldings mark the boundaries of a central zone painted with detached landscapes, groups of rococo ornaments and bouquets of flowers; towards the top, heads in relief, fastened by draperies, support little vases; at the base, above the stem, gadroons in S recall the disposition of certain Italian pieces of the decadence. All this ornamented in soft, well glazed tints, has a very uncommon appearance.

---

* *Histoire de la Céramique.* Paris, 1873.

"A vase equal in merit forms part of the interesting collection of the Comte de Liesville; we will not describe it, the engraving giving the most exact idea of its style and perfection. These last pieces would appear to have been made in the seventeenth century. Specimens of a later date recommend themselves still by their pure enamel, recherché form, and a floral decoration whose soft harmony resembles the polychrome works of Moustiers, with bouquets and wreaths. Would it be also there that was made the bell of the convent in the collection of Arosa where the legend 'Saint Francis pray for us, 1769,' surmounts the view of a village with its churches and towers? Ancient writers speak of a green and white pottery, special to this establishment; we have seen a fine plate, almost of Moresque style, where these colors laid on an engobe formed a rich composition, relieved with graffiti and outlines of manganese."

In the eighteenth century poor imitations of Italian maiolica were made extensively at Talavera, the principal colors employed in the decoration being green, orange, manganese, black and blue. In the collection of the Pennsylvania Museum may be seen several examples of this later period. Illustration 3 represents a low tazza, or dish, the gift of Mrs. John Harrison. The central painting shows a gentleman on horseback, surrounded by foliage, while the border pattern is a foliated scroll design, the colors being yellow, pale green, and light brown.

A characteristic form of the debased style of Talavera ware of the middle or late eighteenth century is the deep, semi-globular bowl, usually embellished in the cavity with a painting of an animal or a heraldic device, and on the outside with a rude landscape or conventional design, the predominating colors being green, yellow and manganese or purple. Two examples of this character are owned by Mrs.

Robert W. de Forest, of New York. One is ornamented with a rudely painted shield inscribed "Biba Jesus," the other with the figure of a dog (illustration 4). In the collection of this Museum a similar bowl, the gift of Mr. John

3. MAIOLICA TAZZA (10¾ Inches).
Yellow, Light Green and Pale Brown.
Talavera, Spain, Eighteenth Century.
In the Museum Collection.

T. Morris, contains the painted representation of a wolf or lion (illustration 5).

From the foregoing quotations we learn that the potters of Talavera were imitating the wares of China in the seventeenth and eighteenth centuries and that as early as the middle of the sixteenth century pottery in several colors was being produced in that place. A hundred years later *azulejos*, or tiles, for the adornment of buildings, gardens and altars, were manufactured to a considerable extent, the term *azulejo* (meaning *blue*) having been applied to the first Delft tiles imported from Holland. The earliest tin glazed tiles of Spain, which superseded the Hispano-Moresque lustered wares, were painted in blue and the name

6. MAIOLICA DISH (14¾ Inches in Height).
Blue Camaieu Decoration.
Genoa, Italy, Eighteenth Century.
In the Museum Collection.
(Compare with Illustration 20.)

has survived until the present time, and is now applied to tiles of all colors.

In the eighteenth century potters went to Spain from Italy and introduced the Italian styles of modeling and painting. It is probable that some of these artisans came from Genoa, as we can trace a marked resemblance in some of the Talavera wares to those of the Italian city. We here show, for purposes of comparison (illustration 6), a fine dish in the Museum collection, with irregular, scalloped

4. MAIOLICA DEEP BOWL.
Decorated in Colors (14 Inches).
Talavera, Spain, Eighteenth Century.
Collection of Mrs. Robert W. de Forest, New York, N. Y.

5. MAIOLICA DEEP BOWL.
Decorated in Colors (14 Inches).
Talavera, Spain, Eighteenth Century.
In the Museum Collection.

edge, bearing the Genoa mark, decorated with a figure scene representing a lady in a chariot, drawn by swans and accompanied by flying cupids, or amorini, painted in blue camaieu.

As we shall see later on, the maiolica and tiles of Mexico were subjected to some of the same influences which left their impress upon the wares of Talavera, and were developed on almost parallel lines.

VIII. THE MAIOLICA OF MEXICO.

The maiolica of Mexico, which reflects the art of Spain, possesses an element of manly vigor in the boldness of its modeling and decorative treatment, which gives it an individuality of its own. Crude and inartistic though it frequently was at the beginning, the refining influence of the Chinese potters made itself felt at a little later date and imparted an elegance to some of the Puebla fabrications which was entirely lacking in the Talavera wares of the same period.

The study of Mexican maiolica reveals the fact that the wares which properly fall under this head are of four different styles, which belong to distinct, but sometimes overlapping, periods of time, as follows:

1st. The Moresque (from about 1575 to 1700).
2d. The Spanish, or Talavera (from about 1600 to 1780).
3d. The Chinese (from about 1650 to 1800).
4th. The Hispano-Mexican, or Pueblan (from about 1800 to 1860).

I. THE MORESQUE STYLE.

The earliest of these styles, of which examples are very scarce, shows unmistakably the Moorish, or Hispano-Moresque, influence and dates from about the latter part of the sixteenth to about the close of the seventeenth century. The so-called Moresque style of decoration is characterized by interlacing scrollwork and strapwork. As early as the fourteenth century the Spanish Moors were producing a peculiar style of wall tiling in which the parallel out-

lines of the designs are in slight relief, forming boundaries
for the enamel colors applied in the grooves between. The
best examples of this variety of tile-work are found in the
Alhambra and throughout southern Spain. This style of
mural decoration was introduced into Mexico probably before the year 1600, and traces of it are yet to be met with
in some of the ecclesiastical edifices of the seventeenth century, notably in the dado of the Chapel of the Rosary
(*Capilla de Nuestra Señora del Rosario*) in the church of Santo
Domingo, Puebla, in which are also sections of strapwork
showing intricate blue and white designs spread over considerable surfaces, repeated at intervals (see illustration 49).
The employment of the Moorish styles of ornamentation
in Mexico may be explained by the fact that previous to
1720 pottery and tiles were exported to New Spain from
various Spanish ports, as we learn from a work published
in Cadiz,* in which, referring to duties and freight on goods
sent to America, it is stated that azulejos (tiles), 5½ inches
square, shall pay, per 1000, 27.12 reales; Geneva tiles, 11
inches square, for paving courts and rooms (evidently unglazed bricks), free; pottery (maiolica) from the factory of
Alcora, free of duties for ten years; pottery from Seville,
free. That these wares were brought into Mexico in considerable abundance for some time previous to 1720, is
doubtless true, and it is equally certain that some of them,
at least, were in the Hispano-Moresque style, which would
have a marked effect on the Mexican productions. The
lavabo, or bowl, of this character, shown in illustration 7,
from the lavatory of the old Mexican convent of San Francisco, at Atlixco, which dates back to the early part of the

---

* *Compendio General de las contribuciones y gastos que ocasionan
todos los Efectos Frutos, Caudales y demas, que se trafican entre los
Reynos de Castilla y America. Deducidas del Real Proyecto de 5 de
Abril de el Año pasado de 1720, etc., etc. Cadiz, 1762.*

seventeenth century, is covered with a handsome scrollwork design in blue, outlined with black. The central pattern is purely Moorish in spirit, both in composition and coloring,

7. MAIOLICA LAVABO (20 Inches).
Decorated in Blue, Outlined in Black.
Showing Moorish Influence.
Puebla, About 1650. From an old Convent.
In the Museum Collection.

variations of this treatment being still employed by the modern Moorish potters. The question has been raised whether this piece was made in Mexico or was brought from Spain. A careful examination of the workmanship clearly shows that it differs from native Moorish work in the treatment of the colors, the blue being thick and standing out in perceptible relief, which was a marked characteristic of the Mexican ware of that and the following century.

II. THE SPANISH, OR TALAVERA STYLE.

It is a popular belief throughout Mexico that potters were brought from Talavera, Spain, by the Dominican Friars, who reached New Spain in 1526. Just when the first importation of maiolists into Mexico occurred is somewhat uncertain, but, as we shall presently see, it could not have been much later than the middle of the sixteenth century. They established potteries in Puebla and initiated the natives into the mysteries of the manufacture, preparing the way for the building up of a great industry which was destined to supply the remarkable tile-work which was used so extensively in the following centuries in the interiors and exteriors of churches, convents, monasteries, hospitals and private dwellings.

According to Consul-General A. M. Gottschalk,* of Mexico City, the first potters and tile-makers brought from Spain were artisan members of a religious order. "The history of the Puebla 'Talavera' ware," he writes, "appears to be as follows: In the early days of Puebla's history the Dominican friars, struck by the aptitude of their Aztec parishioners at making crude native pottery, and desirous also of obtaining tiles for the monastery and church which they were building, sent word to the Dominican establishment at Talavera de la Reina, in the Province of Toledo, Spain, that they could make good use of five or six of the brotherhood who were acquainted with the Spanish process of pot-

---

* *Daily Consular and Trade Reports,* Washington, D. C., No. 2975, p. 15.

tery making, if such could be sent out to them. Accordingly a number of Dominican friars, familiar with the clay-working processes in use at Talavera, were assigned to the Puebla house of their order, and under them were trained a generation of workmen, who for the first few succeeding years produced some excellent pieces. In course of time the industry was gradually discontinued, and with the confiscation of church property and the withdrawal of the religious orders from Mexico little more than the tradition remained."

While with considerable confidence we assign to the earlier period of maiolica manufacture in Mexico those pieces which reflect the Mauresque feeling in decorative treatment, we find that at a little later date, if not contemporaneously, was produced a Hispanized style of pottery in Mexico, in which the Italian influence can be traced, but which we now know as the Talavera style. As Talavera is in the interior of Spain, its pottery shows less of Moorish influence than that of Malaga or Valencia on the Mediterranean coast. Consequently the Talavera pottery presents certain resemblances to some of the Italian maiolica, particularly that of Savona and Genoa. It is known that potters and decorators went to Talavera from Italy in the seventeenth century, and it is therefore not surprising that the Italian influence should be strongly marked in the Talavera wares of that period. The characteristics of the earlier Talavera maiolica are an absence of metallic lustres, which were so prominent a feature in the products of Malaga and Valencia, and the prevalence of blue color in the white enamel of the ground. Animal, bird and human forms were introduced, in combination with foliated and floriated ornaments, frequently crowded together without regard to position or fitness. In illustration 2 we have shown a plate or shallow dish of this character, belonging to the early part of the eighteenth century, which was recently obtained in Spain for this Museum. The decorations, in dark blue, are strongly suggestive of some of the Puebla work of the same period and reveal one of the sources from which the Mexican potters derived their inspiration.

8. MAIOLICA BOWL (15 Inches).
Blue Decoration. Showing Spanish Influence.
Puebla, About 1685.
In the Museum Collection.

The earliest examples of Talavera style made in Mexico are probably those in which the ornamentation is tattooed, or rudely painted in dots and dashes in dark blue. This class of work is found on tiles, bowls, albarelli, or so-called apothecary jars, barrel-shaped vases, or jardinieres, spherical jars (imitating the ginger jars of China), and occasionally on other objects. Of bowls there were many varieties and sizes, but one of the best which has thus far come to light is the large, shallow specimen shown in illustration 8, in which the birds and hare are distinctly Talaveran, while the Moorish influence crops out in the three mosque-shaped buildings.

9. MAIOLICA BOWL (10½ Inches Diam.).
Blue Decoration.
Showing Spanish Influence.
Puebla, About 1680.
In the Museum Collection.

This interesting piece is supposed to have been produced previous to the year 1700, at the time when both the Moresque and Talavera influences were at work in Puebla. Most characteristic of the tattooed style is the bowl shown in illustration 9. In illustration 10 we see an urn-shaped flower vase, or jardiniere, of this style, bearing on the side the word BERNAL, the name of the family for which it was originally made. This example is owned by Señor

Rafael Cervantes, of Mexico. A fine example is shown in illustration 11. It is a bowl, upwards of twenty inches in diameter and six and a half inches in depth, owned by Mr. Albert Pepper. In place of connected lines to represent flowers and foliage, the artist has used successions and groupings of small dots, made with the point of the brush,

10. MAIOLICA URN-SHAPED JARDINIERE.
Decorated in Blue.
Showing Spanish Influence.
Puebla, About 1680.
Collection of Señor Rafael Cervantes.

with rows of coarse lines, to represent the costume of the figure. To give detail to certain parts, as the face and hands of the figure, these important features have been outlined in pale blue. This may be termed the impressionistic style of maiolica painting, which requires distance to bring out the significance and harmony of the design. At close range we see what appear to be detached rattles of serpents, a confused assemblage of meaningless dots, filling in all of the white spaces, interspersed with dashes and blotches of blue color. Careful study, however, reveals an ingenious arrangement of the motives, in which foliage and flowers

11.   MAIOLICA BASIN (20¼ Inches).
Decorated in Blue.
Showing Spanish Influence.
Puebla, About 1680.
Collection of Mr. Albert Pepper.

are plainly distinguishable, with here and there a long-tailed bird in flight, a wriggling fish or other creature of the air, or land, or water. The border design of the bowl, on close inspection, will be found to consist of a series of well-defined panel devices, separated by leaf-like ornaments. A vase of Chinese form, twenty inches in height, decorated in the

12. MAIOLICA VASE.
Blue Decoration.
Showing Spanish Influence.
Puebla, About 1680.

Talavera manner, is completely covered around the upper portion with crowded paintings of foliage and flowers, houses, a sail boat or pinnace, and figures of men, squirrels, birds, and deer (see illustration 12).

One of the most characteristic styles of decoration, found frequently on albarelli and spherical jars, is that in which birds, flowers and conventional devices are boldly but rudely painted in silhouette, or solid, raised dark blue, almost entirely covering the white surface (see illustration 13).

Examples of Mexican maiolica of the seventeenth and eighteenth centuries, in the Talavera style, are compara-

13. MAIOLICA JARS (10 and 9 Inches in Height).
Blue Decoration.
Showing Spanish Influence.
Puebla, 1700-1750.

tively abundant, and will be found in every collection of this ware. The albarelli, which in Italy were almost exclusively devoted to the uses of the apothecary, were later, in Mexico, employed largely as receptacles for flowers, and rarely, if ever, bear the names of drugs, although some of them possess a plain white band which extends diagonally across one side, evidently intended to furnish a reserved space for a label. Several examples of these cylindrical jars, in the Museum collection, strongly reveal the Spanish feeling, both in form and decorative treatment. In illustration 15 five of these, dating back to about 1700-1750, are shown. These jars were generally made with projecting flanges at the base, after an old Spanish form, which were intended to fit

14. MAIOLICA JAR (10½ Inches).
Blue Decoration.
With Iron Cover, Lock and Key.
Showing Spanish Influence in Decoration,
And Chinese Influence in Form and Metal Work.
Puebla, About 1700.
In the Museum Collection.

into holes or sockets in a wooden shelf, to hold the vessels in place, but this practice does not seem to have been followed in Mexico. Consequently we find examples of this form with smooth, flat bottoms, in addition to those with the projecting foot, or basal ring.

Inkstands and sand-shakers appear to have been produced in large numbers, about the middle of the eighteenth

16. MAIOLICA INKSTANDS.
Decorated in Blue.
Showing Spanish Influence.
Puebla, About 1750.
In the Museum Collection.

17. MAIOLICA INKSTANDS.
a. Decorated in Colors, About 1800.
b. Decorated in Blue, About 1750.
In the Museum Collection.

century, since many examples are to be found in collections
(see illustration 16).* The usual form of the older examples

---

* Blue and white ink wells of this type have been found in the
islands to the eastward, several hundred miles from Puebla, evidences
of the traffic which was carried on between Mexico and the West
Indies in the eighteenth century.

15. MAIOLICA DRUG JARS (ALBARELLI), OR FLOWER VASES.
Decorated in Blue.
Showing Spanish Influence.
Puebla, 1700-1750.
The Upper Pair are in the Museum Collection.

is hexagonal, the ornamentation consisting of dots and small details rudely applied to the sides. Occasionally a more elaborate form was attempted, such as the large specimen shown in illustration 17.

The widespread belief which today prevails throughout Mexico that Talavera in Spain was the source from which the art was derived has resulted in the general adoption of the term "Talavera" for all tin enameled pottery which has been produced, or found, in the land of the Aztecs. This broad use of the name, however, while in a manner correct, is misleading, since, as we have already stated, there are several distinct styles of this stanniferous faience which reached their final development through entirely different channels.

III. THE CHINESE STYLE.

A large proportion of Puebla maiolica made during the latter half of the seventeenth, and throughout the greater part of the eighteenth century, reflects, in form and decorations, the methods of the Chinese potters. We have already referred to the claim of certain Mexican antiquaries that Chinese or Japanese workmen were brought to Mexico, presumably from the Philippine Islands, for the purpose of manufacturing this ware. This theory is unsupported by fact, as it is very evident to the expert that the pseudo-Chinese decorations of the Mexican wares were not executed by Oriental artists. On the contrary, they plainly show the bungling efforts of Spanish or Mexican decorators to imitate Chinese work. No piece has yet been discovered which reveals the unmistakable hand of an Oriental decorator.

Commercial relations between the Philippines and New Spain were established fully as early as 1600, when trading galleons began to sail between Luzon and Mexico. From

"The Earliest Historical Relations Between Mexico and Japan," by Mrs. Zelia Nuttall, published by the University Press of Berkeley, California (1906), we quote the following passages:

"More or less frequent indirect intercourse between Japan and Mexico undoubtedly took place as soon as communication was established between the Philippine Islands and Acapulco (Mexico).

"In 1608 there were fifteen thousand Japanese residing in the Philippines, some of whom were probably employed in the crews of the galleons, eight of which came to Acapulco each year. In 1610, with the ex-governor of the Philippines, Vivero, twenty-three Japanese noblemen and merchants spent five months in Mexico and its capital.

"In 1613, one hundred and eighty Japanese spent four and a half months in Mexico. The majority remained when the embassy departed for Europe, seventy-eight returning to Acapulco. The presumption is that they remained there awaiting the return of the ambassadors, which was delayed for six years.

"Iyemitsu's prohibition to Japanese to leave their country, under penalty of death, indicates that a large number of persecuted Christians had been going into voluntary exile. In all probability some of these, and also members of the Japanese colony in the Philippines, came to Mexico and settled there.

.   .   .   .

"It is obvious, therefore, that it is the first duty of ethnologists to assign to the above influx of Japanese into Mexico in historical times any indications of Asiatic influence that they may detect, and for anthropologists to consider the more or less limited mingling of races which doubtless occurred in the seventeenth century and afterwards.

"I will set an example by attributing to the Japanese who visited Mexico in the seventeenth century the introduction of the rain-coat made of grass or palm leaves, which is worn by the Indians inhabiting the Pacific coast of Mexico, and which is said to be identical with that used in Japan from time immemorial. . . . .

"The practical lesson thus taught the observant natives and the models furnished by the rain-coats discarded at the end of the wet season would surely sufficiently account for the introduction and use to the present day of these useful and easily manufactured garments, of which a specimen, bought in the market-place at Oaxaca, has been sent by the writer to the Museum of the Department of Anthropology of the University of California."

From the above quotations we learn that the Japanese began to impress their influence upon some of the manufacturers of Mexico at the beginning of the seventeenth century, although the art of pottery making does not appear to have received any impulse from that source. It was through China, which, at a little later period, commenced to ship her wares, through the same port of Acapulco, into Mexico, that the Asiatic influence began to affect the ceramic industry of New Spain, not directly through her own skilled artisans, but indirectly through the extensive influx of her finest porcelains. This inference is unavoidable when a careful study of the maiolica of Mexico reveals no trace of Japanese suggestion.

The importation of this ware into Mexico in such large quantities naturally stimulated the artistic zeal of the native potters, who soon commenced to imitate the Eastern forms and decorations in their own productions. The spherical jar-shaped vase with bell-shaped cover was extensively copied, and it will be found that the greater number of such pieces are ornamented with characteristic motives and en-

tire designs derived from the Chinese (see illustration 21).
These jars are made in many sizes, some of which are ex-
ceedingly capacious. In the lapse of time most of the dome-
shaped lids, belonging to the Mexican maiolica, have been
broken or lost, so that it is only occasionally that an ancient
jar is found with cover intact. Among the Oriental porcelain vases of this form found in Mexico many were provided
with hinged iron lids having a lock and key for the safe
keeping of ginger and other confections. Some of the
Puebla jars were mounted with metal covers in the same
manner, in which chocolate and vanilla could be safely
locked. In illustration 14 we show a jar of this character,
which, while Chinese in shape, is decorated in Spanish style.
The iron collar and lid are purely Oriental. The head of
the key is wrought in an openwork design representing an
animal.

There are four distinct varieties of decorative work in
the Chinese style, which probably emanated from as many
different factories, and these are almost invariably painted
in blue monochrome, or camaieu, as follows:

1st. The variety with blue ground and designs reserved in white.
2d. Chinese figure decorations.
3d. European figure decorations, usually combined with Oriental
motives.
4th. The white medallion variety with conventionalized floral
decorations.

The first variety is exemplified in those tiles on which
the details have been outlined in pale blue, the background
having afterwards been rudely filled in with thick blue pigment, leaving the patterns reserved in white (see lower
pair in illustration 40). Many examples of these tiles may
be seen in the Museum collection. One shows a conventionalized bird (illustration 39); another the figure of a China-

man carrying a fan, both taken from a house dated 1687, while two specimens,—a square tile and an angle tile,—are decorated with wingéd cherubs (illustration 39). A vase owned by Mr. Albert Pepper (illustration 18) is a good ex-

18. MAIOLICA VASE (14 Inches in Height).
White Decoration Reserved in Blue Ground.
Showing Chinese Influence.
Puebla, 1650-1700.
Collection of Mr. Albert Pepper.

ample of this class, although it also possesses the characteristics of the fourth variety.

The second style is characterized by blue figure paintings in Chinese manner, on a white ground. In illustration 19 is shown an interesting example which combines the first and second styles. The decoration is divided into eight vertical panels with these two styles alternating.

One of the finest pieces in the collection of this Museum is a large jar-shaped vase of Chinese form, painted in blue camaieu (see illustration 20), which is remarkable as re-

19. MAIOLICA VASE (15 Inches in Height).
Decorated in Blue.
Showing Chinese Influence.
Puebla, 1650-1700.

flecting in its decoration the art of Italy, through Spain, in combination with Oriental figure motives. It was purchased with money contributed by Mrs. John Harrison. We recognize in the excellence of the drawing, particularly of the chariot, a suggestion of the Italian style, as in a blue and white dish in the Museum collection, which bears the mark

20. MAIOLICA VASE.
Decorated in Blue Camaieu (18½ Inches in Height).
The Chariot and Horses Reflect the Italian Taste.
The Driver Shows Chinese Influence.
Puebla, About 1660.
Presented by Mrs. John Harrison.

of Genoa (see illustration 6). Another jar-shaped vase in the collection is encircled by irregular medallions with pseudo-Chinese designs (see illustration 21). Were it not for the Oriental figures occupying the white medallions we would class

21. MAIOLICA VASE (13 Inches in Height).
Blue Decoration.
Showing Chinese Influence.
Puebla, About 1700.
In the Museum Collection.

this vase with the fourth variety. Frequently two or more of the Oriental styles are found in combination, which would seem to indicate that certain factories, which did not originate a distinctive style, appropriated some of the prominent peculiarities of other wares and united them in their own.

This is the case with an enormous tub, or cistern, which combines the first, second and third styles, and is the largest piece of this ware at present known (see illustration 22). Oval in

22. MAIOLICA BATH TUB, OR CISTERN.
(24 Inches High, 40 Inches Long.)
Decorated in Blue and Brown.
Showing Chinese and Spanish Influences.
Puebla, About 1650-1680.

form, it stands twenty-four inches in height, measures forty inches in length, and is elaborately ornamented in blue and white over its entire outside surface, around the upper por-

23. MAIOLICA BASIN.
Decorated in Blue (20½ Inches).
Figures Outlined in Brown.
Showing Chinese Influence.
Puebla, About 1660.
In the Museum Collection.

tion of the interior and in the bottom. The figure designs, enclosed in irregular medallions, represent Chinamen mounted on horses, apparently beating drums, and Spaniards

24. MAIOLICA JARDINIERE (16 Inches in Height).
Decorated in Blue.
Showing Chinese Influence.
Puebla, About 1750.
Collection of Mrs. Robert W. de Forest.

shooting deer. At the base of each of the broad sides are towers of churches. Around the outside are four heads of bulls in bold relief, two at each side, and at each end a

modeled cow's head. These are colored brown and serve
the purpose of handles. The peculiar style of the painting,
in which the figures are outlined in dark brown, would seem
to indicate a common origin for this and a large tub-shaped
basin in the Museum collection (see illustration 23), which
in form is distinctly Spanish, while the blue ornamentation,

25. MAIOLICA BARREL-SHAPED JARDINIERES.
Blue Decoration.
Showing Chinese Influence.
Puebla, About 1750.
Collection of Señor Rafael Cervantes.

consisting of figures, outlined in dark brown, shows Chinese influence. A Chinaman, with raised umbrella, is
mounted on a horse, two Chinamen are flying a kite, while
a fourth, also holding an umbrella, is painted beneath.
Four parrots are perched on a nopal, or cactus. On the
under side of this extraordinary piece appear the initials
C. S., painted in blue (see chapter on Marks). Frequently
we find a vessel of Chinese shape, bearing decorative designs

in Spanish style, and occasionally the two varieties of painting are combined.

The third variety of ornamentation, in which the Chinese influence is strongly marked, is that in which European

26. MAIOLICA BOWL AND VASE.
Blue Decoration.
Showing Chinese Influence.
Puebla, About 1760.

figures and animals have been painted in imitation of Oriental work. These paintings remind us of the work of Oriental artists which distinguishes a variety of Chinese porcelain, sometimes known as "Lowestoft," or "Heraldic" china,
copied from foreign designs, made for the European market.

Special decorations were executed in China for the Mexican trade, including plates and other articles embellished with the double-headed, crowned eagle of the Austrian dynasty. This same heraldic emblem is frequently found on tiles and tile panels made in Puebla previous to 1700.   This third style

27.   MAIOLICA VASE (21 Inches in Height).
Blue Decoration.
Showing Chinese Influence.
Puebla, About 1700.

is found at its best on certain tiles which were evidently produced at a single factory.   The figure designs are usually of Spanish type, but the paintings of animals have been apparently adapted from Chinese decorations.   On the faces of many of these tiles will be found the letter F, penciled in blue, in all probability standing for the name of the decorator.   On

other examples, however, are found, among the decorative
details, a fly or bee, which by some collectors has been supposed to stand for the initial B. Several of these tiles are
shown in illustration 41.

28. MAIOLICA VASE.
Decorated in Blue.
Showing Chinese Influence.
Puebla, About 1700.

The fourth variety is distinguished by open medallions
of ornate shapes, in which are floral embellishments, and
which are surrounded by a ground-work of conventional
decorations in blue. Some of these are elegant in concep-
tion and execution and imitate in a creditable manner the

best designs found on their Oriental models. To this class belongs the vase shown in illustration 21, and the large barrel-shaped jardiniere figured in illustration 24, in the collection of Mrs. Robert W. de Forest, of New York.

Other examples of the medallion style are represented in illustration 25, of two large, barrel-shaped flower pots, in the collection of Señor Rafael Cervantes; illustration 26, of a large bowl, made for a Capuchin convent, and a beautiful vase of ginger-jar form; illustration 27, of a vase, twenty-one inches in height, which combines the first and fourth styles; and illustration 28, of a large mortar-shaped vessel with handles. In illustrations 25 and 26 we see examples of the best period of maiolica decoration in Oriental taste.

Mr. Thomas A. Janvier, in his *Mexican Guide,* states that the first members of the Order of Capuchinas in Mexico, coming from a convent of the order in Toledo, Spain, arrived in the Capital of Mexico October 8, 1665, where they erected a convent which was dedicated in 1666. In 1756 the primitive church built by them was replaced by a larger structure, and in 1861 both convent and church were demolished. It is probable that the bowl shown in illustration 26 was made about the time of the completion of the second church building.

IV.   THE HISPANO-MEXICAN, OR PUEBLAN, STYLE.

In the latter half of the eighteenth century polychrome decorations were applied to the Spanish pottery of Talavera, in imitation of Italian maiolica, in which greens, browns, purples and yellows were conspicuous. As we have already seen, a large, deep bowl painted in these colors (see illustration 4) is owned by Mrs. Robert W. de Forest, of New York, and a similar example, ornamented with a central figure of a lion, in purplish brown, is in the collection of this

Museum (see illustration 5). In the same collection is a tazza painted in yellow, light green and pale brown (see

29. MAIOLICA VASE (18 Inches in Height).
Decorated in Polychrome.
Puebla, 1780-1800.
In the Museum Collection.
(See Frontispiece, for Reverse Side).

illustration 3). The coloring of these pieces is characteristic of the degraded Talavera pottery of the later period.

About the beginning of the nineteenth century the Pueblan potters began to develop a style of their own, and materially increased the range of their color scale, so that on ware of this period we find designs in blue, green, yellow, red, brown and black. By this time the Chinese influence had entirely disappeared. Figure painting in gaudy coloring came into vogue. In illustration 29 is shown the

30. MAIOLICA DRUG JARS (8¾ Inches in Height).
Decorated in Natural Colors.
Puebla, About 1830.
In the Museum Collection.

reverse side of the vase represented in the frontispiece. This is one of the best examples of this style that has yet come to light. Two albarelli, one decorated with tulips in red and green, the other with roses in natural colors, are shown in illustration 30.

At a later date other tints were added, such as mauve, or purplish rose. This beautiful color is found on several examples of the ware in this Museum, including a large basin, and a small two-handled bowl (illustration 31), and the ap-

31. MAIOLICA BOWL (7¾ Inches Diam.).
Decorated in Mauve and Green.
Puebla, About 1820.
In the Museum Collection.

32. MAIOLICA COVERED BOWL (9½ Inches Diam.).
Decorated in Mauve, Green and Brown.
Puebla, About 1820.
Collection of Mr. Albert Pepper.

proximate date of its introduction is established by means

of a large covered bowl, in the possession of Mr. Albert Pepper, which bears on one side the inscription "Viva Fernando 7th" (illustration 32). The ornamentation consists of roses painted in this peculiar tone, varied with green. Since

33. MAIOLICA BASIN (20½ Inches).
Decorated in Polychrome.
"The Baptism of the Saviour."
Puebla, About 1800.
Collection of Mr. Albert Pepper.

Ferdinand VII. of Spain reigned from 1808 to 1833, this example probably dates from the first quarter of the nineteenth century and fixes the age of other pieces showing this rare and beautiful color.

The Hispano-Mexican, or Pueblan, style may be said to cover the period from about 1800 to 1860. During this later period were produced salt cellars, benitiers, large cir-

34. MAIOLICA JARDINIERE (18 Inches in Height).
Decorated in Polychrome.
Puebla, About 1800.
In the Museum Collection.

cular dishes, albarelli, flower vases of many forms, cup holders, bowls of various sizes and shapes, articles for toilet use and many other objects of original, and frequently inartistic,

design. A large bowl or basin in the collection of Mr. Albert
Pepper, is embellished with a polychrome painting representing the baptism of the Saviour (illustration 33). An

35. MAIOLICA BASIN (16 Inches).
Decorated in Mauve, Blue and Brown.
"Dancing the Fandango."
Puebla, About 1820.
In the Museum Collection.

artistic flower barrel, in the Museum collection, is adorned
with flowers and foliage in rose color and green (illustration 34). A large bowl, in the same collection, bears a
crudely painted scene intended to portray the dancing of

the fandango, encircled by a handsome border design in blackish brown (illustration 35). In illustration 36 are shown two salt cellars decorated with fishes in yellow and green, and a benitier, or holy water stoup, from a Carmelite convent, bearing the escutcheon of the order, which was es-

36. MAIOLICA SALT CELLARS AND BENITIER.
Polychrome Decorations.
(2¾, 8¾ and 3¼ Inches in Height).
Puebla, About 1830.
The Benitier Bears the Carmelite Arms.
In the Museum Collection.

tablished in Mexico in the year 1585. A salt cellar in red and green, and a cup holder, with decorative designs in delicate shades of mauve and green, the latter in the collection of Mr. Albert H. Pitkin, of Hartford, Conn., are figured in illustration 37.

Before the middle of the nineteenth century the de-

cadence began. Gaudy and crude colors were much employed and over-decoration vulgarized the ware. About
the year 1860 jugs and other vessels, fashioned in the
forms of hideous heads and grotesque figures, came into
vogue. About this time, or perhaps a few years earlier, a
pale, grayish blue ground color was used extensively on
plates, vases and other pieces, quite similar to that seen
on one variety of Italian drug jars. After that the ware
lost every artistic feature and degenerated into the ordinary

37. MAIOLICA CUP HOLDER AND SALT CELLAR.
Decorated in Colors.
Puebla, About 1830.

commercial product of Puebla and Oaxaca of the present
day.

In addition to tin enameled pottery another variety of
ware was produced to some extent in Mexico, under Spanish influence. We refer to the sgraffito earthenware made
at Guanajuato. This ware is covered with a thin wash, or
engobe, of white clay, glazed with lead. The decorative
devices are scratched through the white slip to show the red
color of the clay beneath, and afterwards touched in places
with green oxide of copper. The process is the same as that
employed by the Italian potters in the sixteenth and seventeenth centuries and is identical with that of the Pennsyl-

vania-German potters of the eighteenth century. A dish of this character, made about 1830, is shown in illustration 38, which is inserted here for the purpose of calling attention to

38. SGRAFFITO DISH (16½ Inches Long).
Lead Glazed.
Showing Spanish or Italian Influence.
Made at Guanajuato, Mexico, About 1830.
In the Museum Collection.

an entirely distinct art, which was introduced at a later period by the Spanish potters. The decorative color effects were obtained by engraving, instead of painting, thus utilizing the natural colors of the clay, red and yellow.

IX. The Tin Enameled Tiles of Mexico.

It is probable that the first maiolica tiles used for mural decoration in Mexico were brought from Spain, but before the close of the sixteenth century the tile industry became well established in Puebla and the native tile-makers from that time on were abundantly able to fill the requirements of the home market. Not only did they produce geometrical and conventional patterns of great variety (at first in blue and later in polychrome), but they employed competent artists who painted pictures and figure subjects on large panels composed of numerous small tiles, for insertion in the exterior and interior walls of buildings. A square or panel of four or five inch white tiles, consisting frequently of seven rows of five each, and often of a greater number, occasionally as many as one hundred and fifty being combined in a single design, was treated as a canvas, on which the picture was painted in vitrifiable colors. The set of small tiles could then be separated for transportation and put together again in the place for which it was designed. Figures of saints, of varying degrees of excellence, were painted for ecclesiastical edifices, and some of these have fallen into the hands of appreciative persons who have set them in the walls of their houses. Illustration 47 represents a panel showing the Virgin of Guadalupe, at the base of which are two cups for holy water. The colors are subdued and harmonious, the border design of roses being executed in their natural tints. This panel, though of much more recent date, has been set in the wall of the passage leading from the patio to the garden behind the Casa de

39. MAIOLICA TILES.
Blue Ground, Design Reserved in White.
Showing Spanish and Chinese Influence.
Puebla, 1650-1680.
In the Museum Collection.

Alvarado, in Coyoacán, near the City of Mexico, which was erected by Alvarado, one of the conquistadors, about 1521, and is now occupied by Mrs. Zelia Nuttall, the eminent archæologist.

The native Puebla tiles used for interior wall decoration are found to be of practically uniform size, about four and three-quarters to five inches square, almost invariably slightly curved or convex, and beveled on the edges, so that they could be used indiscriminately for flat or rounded surfaces, such as columns, etc. (see illustration 58). On the upper surface of a majority of the Puebla tiles may be seen three rough spots, varying in size from that of a pin's head to that of a pea, arranged in the form of a triangle,—the scars left by the cockspurs or clay supports used to separate the pieces in the kiln. In addition to these features the dark blue color of the Mexican tiles is always in perceptible relief, an effect caused by the thickness of this pigment. Of thousands of Puebla tiles, from various places and of many periods, examined by the writer, there was scarcely one which did not possess some or all of these characteristics. These peculiarities are so marked that the collector will have no difficulty in distinguishing the Mexican from the Spanish, or Talavera, productions of the same period, which latter are usually somewhat larger in size, painted in flat colors and usually devoid of the three rough kiln marks. Señor Joseph Font y Guma, of Barcelona, Spain, author of "Rajolas Valencianas y Catalanas," who has given much time to the study of Spanish tiles, states that as a general rule they are flat, but some are slightly curved, owing to accidental warping in drying or baking. The oldest tiles of Valencia, while perfectly level on the surface, were made with beveled edges. At the beginning of the sevententh century the edges became less beveled and at length were made at right angles. Those from Manises, as well as the Andalusian and Castilian tiles, are perfectly flat and without the sloping edges. This writer figures in his book on tiles several examples which bear a striking resemblance to some of those found in the old churches of Puebla.

The Mexican tiles used for exterior embellishment are not so uniform in size, some of them reaching the dimensions of eight or more inches. These are often found in the panels and borders of façades. In addition to the standard tiles for perpendicular surfaces will be found corner or angle tiles, large, square, curved tiles for facing pillars, mouldings for cornices, and numerous forms of architectural ornaments and modeled figures, for roofs, domes, minarets and pilasters.

Little is known of the history of the early tile manufactories of Puebla. That they were numerous may be inferred from the great variety of divergent styles shown in the tiles which have been preserved. Among the earliest are those blue and white tiles, some of which date back to about 1575, with conventional and geometrical patterns, in Talavera style. A group of interesting tiles, examples of which are figured in illustration 40, exhibits a variety of animal and plant motives, in the tattooed style, and shows what spirited effects can be obtained by a few bold strokes of the brush. In this style of work the rabbit, or hare, is frequently represented, in various attitudes, occasionally suggestive of the kangaroo, standing on two legs (see illustration 8). This animal motive is also found on the early Spanish tiles. Some of those produced between 1650 and 1700 reflect strongly the Chinese taste, by means of painting of mandarins, cherubs and birds, rudely reserved in white on a brilliant, dark blue ground (illustrations 39 and 40). Belonging to another class of about the same period are those tiles which are evidently the product of a single factory, bearing animal and figure designs in medium blue on a white ground,—

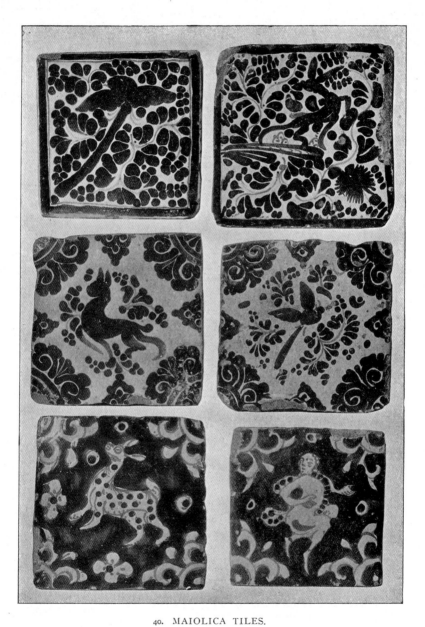

40. MAIOLICA TILES.
In Dark Blue.
The Upper and Middle Pair Show the Tattooed Style.
The Lower Pair, in Chinese Taste, have Dark Blue Ground, with Figures Reserved
in White.
Puebla, 1650-1700.
In the Museum Collection.

41. MAIOLICA TILES.
Painted in Blue.
In Combined Spanish and Chinese Taste.
Some are Signed with the Letter F, Others with the Figure of a Bee.
Puebla, 1650-1700.

dromedaries, elephants, horses, stags, wolves, dogs, boar hunts, bull fights, and figures of saints,*—painted apparently by the same artist, in combined Spanish and Chinese manner, many of which are signed on their faces with the

42.   MAIOLICA TILE.
Decorated in Blue.
Figure of Santa Rosa de Lima.
From an Old Cemetery Near Puebla.
Puebla, 1650-1700.
In the Museum Collection.

letter F., probably the initial of the decorator (see illustration 41).

While the great majority of the tile designs of Puebla

---

* Santa Rosa de Lima, who is supposed to be represented on the tile shown in illustration 42, was born in Peru in 1586 and died in 1617.   Dr. Robert H. Lamborn, in his "Mexican Painting and Painters," refers to her as "the only born American canonized saint." She "was duly enrolled among the saints in 1671 by Clement X., it having been juridically proven by one hundred and eighty witnesses that several miracles were wrought by her means."   A beautiful portrait of Santa Rosa, painted on copper, is in the Lamborn collection of Mexican paintings in this Museum.

show in an unmistakable manner a Spanish or Chinese
origin, a curious exception has been noted in a series of
blue and white tiles recently acquired by this Museum,
which reveal, in a marked degree, the influence of early
Aztec art and may be the work of a native Indian decorator.
These examples are painted with figures of birds, animals,
men and women and human heads, in a few bold strokes and

43.   MAIOLICA TILE.
Decorated in Blue.
Showing Aztec Influence.
Puebla, 1650-1700.
In the Museum Collection.

series of heavy dots, the outlined heads bearing a striking
resemblance to those found in ancient Mexican codices.
Some of these tiles are shown at the bottom of illustration
44. As will be seen, the profiles and costumes are distinctly
Aztec in type. Special attention is called to the curious
example figured in illustration 43, which reveals an attempt
to caricature an Indian, with enormous head, surmounted
by a grotesque bonnet and supported by dwarf-like legs.

And last came the polychrome productions, in which

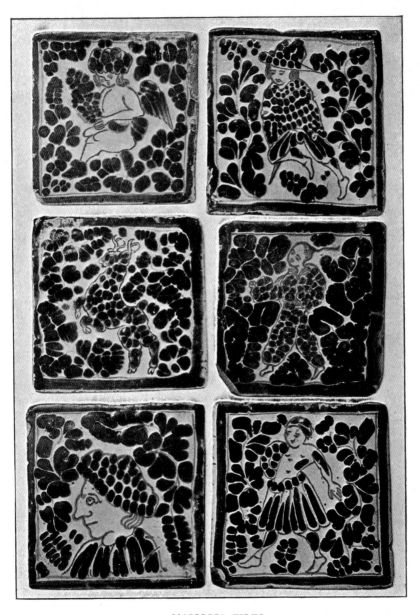

44. MAIOLICA TILES.
Painted in Blue.
The Upper Pair Reveal Spanish Influence, the Middle Pair are in Chinese Style,
while the Lower Ones Reflect Aztec Art.
Puebla, 1650-1700.

yellow, green, brown, mauve, and blue are most prominent, in close imitation of the later Spanish productions, which are to be seen in the old churches of Cuba and other insular possessions of Spain. After the decadence had set in, these polychrome tile paintings rapidly lost their artistic and imitative qualities, finally degenerating into the crudest daubs of unskilled workmen.

The lavish use of tin enameled tiles, in rich colorings, is a striking architectural feature of Mexico. Previous to the year 1600 there were many churches, convents, and other religious foundations, public houses, and private residences whose interiors and exteriors were often literally covered with mosaic patterns in glazed tiles, many of which are yet standing, with their original tile-work still in place. Through the country surrounding Puebla, at the foot of the snow-capped volcano, Popocatepetl, are scores of ancient churches, whose tile-covered domes and towers may be seen from a long distance glistening in the sun. It is to these early structures that we must look for evidences of the antiquity of the tile industry in Mexico.

The convent of San Francisco, at Atlixco, which is believed to date back to about 1575, still contains some of the tiles which were placed there at the time of its construction. In 1604 the Carmelite convent of San José was founded in Puebla although it was not dedicated until 1622. In a book written by Dr. José Gomez de la Parra and printed in that city in 1732,* it is stated that the central part was tiled, with a cupola in each of its four corners and a font of tiles with its basin of stone work in the centre. Quoting from page 83 of the same work, "But let us not leave the choir without noticing the stalls of the nuns, which are

---

* *Fundacion y Primer Siglo del muy religioso convento de Sr. S. Joseph de Religiosas Carmelitas Descalzas de la Ciudad de la Puebla de los Angeles,* etc., p. 79.

certain benches of tiles with the bottoms and backs made of wood," and on the same page mention is made of a staircase of tiles.

The present Cathedral of Puebla, built in the Spanish Renaissance style, was begun about 1550, and was consecrated in 1649, as we learn from a publication which appeared in that year in Puebla, entitled "Sermon sobre la dedicacion de la Catedral de Puebla, por el Lic. Diego Ramirez Grimaldo," the façade not being finished, however, until 1664, while other portions of the building were not completed until later. The dome is enriched with yellow and green tile mosaics representing large circles enclosing many pointed stars, and the domes and lanterns (*cimborios*) capping the towers are encrusted with tiles in red and yellow.

Among the more important structures in Puebla decorated with tile-work, is the church of Guadalupe, which was erected about the middle of the eighteenth century. The surface of the façade is almost entirely encrusted with tile-work. In the spandrels are figures of flying angels, with yellow garments and orange wings, while the intervening surface of the façade is decorated with zigzag bands in blue, green, orange and white. The tiles at the bases of the towers are green and red, with pictured panels representing the sun and moon with orange bodies and yellow rays, on a blue ground. Beneath these are four larger panels in colored tiles illustrating the legend of the apparition of the Virgin Mary of Guadalupe. They are signed J. H. E. The inscription running through these panels, beginning with the lower left hand corner and reading upward and then down the other side, is "NON FECIT TALITER OMNE NATIONI" (illustration 45). The last panel of the series is shown in the accompanying colored plate.

The legend, as given by several of the earlier chroniclers, runs as follows:

45. FAÇADE OF THE CHURCH OF GUADALUPE.
Puebla, About 1750.
Showing Tile Panels, Illustrating the Legend of the Apparition of the
Virgin of Guadalupe.

Two or three miles from the City of Mexico, where now is the suburb of Guadalupe, is a small mountain called Tepeyácac. On December 9th, of the year 1531, at early dawn, an Indian named Juan Diego, recently converted to the Roman Catholic faith, was passing by this place on his way to mass, and when he had reached the top of the hill he heard the singing of angels and beheld a shining cloud surrounded by a rainbow, in the midst of which appeared a beautiful lady who announced to him that she was the Virgin Mary and directed him to go to the bishop and tell him that it was her will that a temple should be erected in her honor on that spot. The Indian, as instructed, went at once to the palace of the prelate, Señor Don Juan de Zumárraga, and related what he had seen. The bishop received the story with incredulity and Juan Diego, returning to the place where he had seen the apparition found the beautiful lady there awaiting him. He announced the result of his visit and was charged to repair to the bishop a second time and repeat the message. On the ensuing Sunday the Indian again went to mass. After the service he made a second visit to the bishop's palace and repeated his story. The prelate was much impressed with what he had heard, but requested the messenger to return once more with some definite sign that the command was from the Mother of God. Going back to the mountain, Juan Diego reported what the bishop had said to him and he was ordered to come again on the next day for the sign which would be given to him. The serious illness of his uncle prevented the Indian from appearing at the appointed time, but on the following day, December 12th, as he was passing near that place in search of a confessor, the Lady again stood before him. Telling her of his urgent errand she bade him take no further thought of his uncle's illness, as already he had been cured. She then instructed him to cut some flowers in that barren place, which, much to his surprise, he found growing there. This he did and after she had blessed them and arranged them in his tilma, or blanket, the Virgin told him this was the sign that the bishop had demanded.

Juan Diego waited patiently before the palace until the Bishop appeared and when he opened his tilma the flowers fell out and the image of the Holy Virgin was seen painted on the garment. On his return to his home Juan Diego found his uncle cured of his fever, even as the Virgin had declared to him, and on the spot where the Lady had appeared to the Indian the Bishop caused a chapel to be erected. This is believed by the people to be the true story of the apparition of the Holy Maria de Guadalupe, and to this day the miraculous painting is preserved in the church at Guadalupe.

The façade of the church of Nuestra Señora de la Luz contains eight tile panels, the four larger of which represent, in yellow, blue, green and brown, Santa Ana, Saint Joachim, San José de la Luz, and La Santisima Madre de la Luz, respectively. The four secondary panels are painted in polychrome, with a fountain, a well, a pine tree and a palm. The construction of this church was commenced in 1761 and it is probable that it was not completed until several years later. The tile-work, therefore, belongs to the latter part of the eighteenth century.

The ancient convent of Santa Rosa, finished in 1698, is extensively ornamented with glazed paneling, the walls of the patio and kitchen, in particular, presenting a great variety of tile designs (illustration 48).

The church of Santo Domingo in Puebla contains some of the most beautiful examples of tile-work in Mexico. Over the inside of the gateway leading from the street to the courtyard is a tile panel with figure of Saint Michael (San

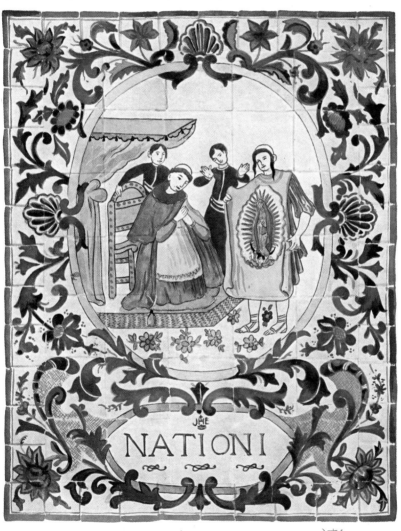

TILE PANEL
In Façade of Church of Guadalupe
Puebla, Mexico, Eighteenth Century

47. MAIOLICA TILE PANEL.
Painted in Polychrome.
"The Virgin of Guadalupe."
Puebla, About 1800.
In the Patio of the Casa de Alvarado, Coyoacán, Mexico.

48. DETAIL OF THE DADO IN THE PATIO OF THE CONVENT OF
SANTA ROSA.
Puebla, About 1698.

49. SECTION OF TILE DADO IN THE CHAPEL OF THE ROSARY, CHURCH OF SANTO DOMINGO.

Puebla, About 1690.

Showing Moorish Influence.

The Cherubs' Heads at the Top are in Relief and in Colors.

Between them are the Escutcheons of Saint Dominic.

50. PORTION OF TILE DADO AND HOLY WATER FONT.
Decorated in Blue.
In Church of Santo Domingo, Puebla, About 1690.
In the Upper Corners of the Picture may be seen the Escutcheon of the Franciscan
Order.

Miguel) inscribed "QUIS UT DEOS." In the chapel of
the Rosary belonging to this church is a dado of blue and
white tile-work about four feet in height, showing Moorish
influence, bordered at the top by a band of modeled tiles
with cherubs' heads in bold relief and beautiful coloring,
alternating with the arms of St. Dominic (Santo Domingo),
in black and white (illustration 49). Adjoining at the right
are sections of relief tile designs in Moresque style, somewhat
similar to some of the tile-work in the Alhambra. Near the
entrance of the church a handsome holy water font, in
enameled blue and white pottery, is set in the dado of tiling
(illustration 50). The exterior of the dome of the chapel is
trimmed with bands and columns of glazed tile, while modeled figures of angels of the same material surmount the
spaces over the windows. The chapel of the Rosary was so
elaborately decorated with tile-work, gilded carvings and
paintings that it was called the eighth wonder of the world.
A work published in Puebla in 1690, entitled "Sermon de la
Dedicacion de la Capilla del Rosario, Su Autor Dr. Diego
Victoria Salazar," seems to prove beyond question that this
chapel was finished in that year. There also appeared in
the same year in Puebla another work entitled "La Octava
Maravilla Capilla del Rosario, Sin Autor," which means
that this work describing the eighth wonder of the world,
the chapel of the Rosary, was published anonymously.

An examination of the tile-work in the chapel of the
Rosary shows beyond question that the dado was constructed when the chapel was originally decorated, so that
we may safely assume that these tiles were made previous to
the year 1690. They are in blue and white and undoubtedly
of Puebla work of that period, as they possess the irregular,
curved surfaces, so characteristic of the Mexican products.
It is also highly probable that the relief border tiles showing cherubs' heads are of the same age, as there seems to
be no evidence that these were inserted at a later date.

The church of San José, erected about the middle of the eighteenth century, is also rich in old Puebla tile-work. At the portal are columns and pilasters, four below and four above, which are faced with glazed tiles in diagonal and zigzag stripes,—yellow, white and blue,—while the dome of the adjoining chapel is also covered with mosaic tile-work (see illustration 51).

In the brick façade of the church of San Francisco (commenced in 1667) are fourteen panels of tile-work representing vases filled with flowers (illustration 52). A band extending across the front, at each side of the doorway, is composed of eight-inch tiles with polychrome paintings representing animals and birds in colors, beneath which is a border of grotesque masks or heads painted in green and yellow (illustration 53). Two of these tiles with figures of a bull and parrot may be seen in the Museum collection. Sylvester Baxter states that the façade belongs to the eighteenth century. In the lavatory of this church until recently stood a handsome lavabo of tiles, decorated with floral designs and bearing the escutcheon of the Franciscan monks (illustration 54), which order arrived in Mexico about 1524.

Other structures in Puebla which are beautified by native tile-work are the church of Carmen, built in the eighteenth century, with gateway surmounted by a pictured panel representing a crowned Virgin and Child; the church of Nuestra Señora de la Soledad, of the same period, built in the Spanish Renaissance style, with dome covered with black and white tile in geometrical designs; the convent church of Santa Catarina, in the Mudéjar style, with tower completely encrusted with polychrome tiling; the Casa de Alfeñique (The House of Almond Cake), now a private residence, entirely covered on front and side with geometrical pattern in blue and white tile set in a dull red ground, built in the Churrigueresque style of the late seventeenth century,

51. FRONT OF CHURCH OF SAN JOSÉ, PUEBLA.
Showing Tile Pillars.
Decorated in Polychrome.

52. FACADE OF CHURCH OF SAN FRANCISCO.
Puebla, About 1750.
Showing Tile Panels.

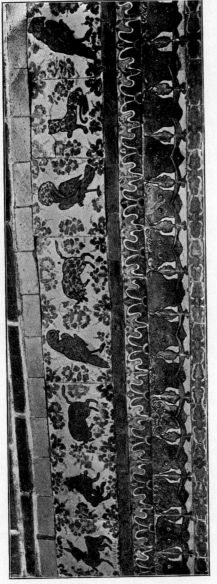

53. PORTION OF TILE FRIEZE IN THE FACADE OF THE CHURCH OF SAN FRANCISCO, PUEBLA.
About 1750.
Eight-inch Tiles with Polychrome Paintings of Birds and Animals
Surmounting a Band of Masks Painted in Yellow and Green.

so-called from its originator, Don Josef Churriguera, a noted Spanish architect; the building now occupied by the Hotel de France, interesting as showing in the front wall sixteen panels containing glazed paintings of grotesque life-size human figures, which are said to have been placed there by the owner of the building in order to annoy the occupants of the structure on the opposite side of the street, who had endeavored to obstruct his efforts to procure permission from the city to make certain additions to the front.

The church of San Miguel el Angel, erected toward the end of the seventeenth century, which passed through many vicissitudes during the Pueblan wars, at one time contained much handsome tile-work. The dado included a series of five-inch tiles, each bearing a painted figure of St. Michael, in various attitudes, colored yellow, orange and black, on a dark blue ground. One of these is shown in the accompanying plate.

In Mexico City, situated a little more than one hundred miles northwest of the Puebla potteries, may still be seen some of the old tiles, but the majority of the buildings which were so decorated have been demolished, and little of the old glazed tile-work remains. The tile-covered dome of the Hotel del Jardin, formerly a convent, was still standing in November, 1907, but it was then reported that the building had recently been sold and that it would soon be razed to make room for a modern structure.

The church of La Santissima Trinidad, in the City of Mexico, built in Churrigueresque style, dates from 1755. On the roof of the dome are large tile panels worked in various designs, one of them showing the keys of Saint Peter and bearing inscriptions.

The principal dome of the church of San Francisco, also in Mexico City (1716-1791), is covered with elaborate tile mosaics.

54. TILE LAVER OF THE CHURCH OF SAN FRANCISCO.
Puebla, About 1750.
With Escutcheon of the Franciscan Monks.

Clara de Puy

MAIOLICA TILE
Figure of San Miguel (St. Michael)
Made in Puebla, Mexico, About 1680

At the corner of the First Calle de San Francisco and the Plazuela de Guardiola stands what is popularly known as the *Casa de los Azulejos* (the House of Tiles) now occupied as the headquarters of the Jockey Club. The original structure was built by the Conde del Valle de Orizaba in the sixteenth century and was remodeled about the middle of the eighteenth. The style of the building is Mudéjar, showing Moorish influence. The front and side are almost entirely covered with tile designs in blue, white and yellow geometrical patterns. The back portion of the edifice was constructed at a later period, and the tile-work, which was intended to match the glazed designs of the front, is of comparatively recent date. Some believe that the older tiles used in the construction of this building are of porcelain and were made in China, but this is manifestly an error which has been disseminated by some of the guide books on Mexico. The writer has examined these tiles carefully and can state without hesitation that they are of the ordinary tin enameled pottery such as was produced at Puebla, about the middle of the eighteenth century. Sylvester Baxter, in his "Spanish-Colonial Architecture in Mexico," states that in the patio the dado of the corridor and staircase are covered with handsome tile patterns, and in the latter, the arms of the house are wrought in colored mosaics.

The Carmelite church and monastery of Nuestra Señora del Carmen at San Angel, dating back to 1628, is a fine example of tile decoration. The interior is beautifully embellished with intricate designs in glazed tile, while the exterior is particularly conspicuous on account of its tiled domes with inlaid figure panels and glazed modeled figures and polychrome minarets. The monastery portion of this structure, which was occupied at one time by about four hundred monks, has fallen into decay, but the church adjoining it is still in use.

At Churubusco the monastery church of Santa Maria de los Angeles (completed in 1678), in Spanish Renaissance style, is still resplendent in its brilliant dress of tile. Particularly interesting are some panel designs, twenty-four inches in height, in the dado of the choir, representing in colors (yellow, green and black) lemon trees laden with fruit, and other trees, interspersed with twenty-six-inch panels with polychrome paintings of Chinese vases on stands (illustration 56). The colors are blue, yellow, green and brown. The chapel of San Antonio Abad adjoining the church is covered with brightly colored tile-work from the bases to the top of the dome. The kneeling effigies of Don Diego del Castillo and his wife, Doña Helena de la Cruz, the patron and patroness of the church and monastery, carved in wood, are still to be seen in niches in the wall.

At Tlaxcala is the famous shrine of the Santuario de Ocotlán, which stands upon a hill about a mile southeast of the plaza. It is built in the Churrigueresque style, and dates from about the middle of the eighteenth century. The front of the church, including the two towers, is encrusted with glazed tile of a dull red color set in white mortar, which, at a distance, presents the peculiar appearance of the laminated markings of a serpent's or shark's skin.

At Querétaro is the church of Santa Clara. The tower and dome are said to have been built about 1607 and reconstructed at the latter end of the eighteenth century. The convent once connected with this church covered several acres of ground and is said to have been occupied at one time by eight thousand nuns. The tower and dome of the church are beautifully decorated with glazed tile in polychrome designs. The church and monastery of San Augustin also show some handsome work in glazed tiles.

The church of San Sebastian and Santa Prisca, at Tasco, dates from the middle of the eighteenth century and is of

56. TILE PANEL.
In the Dado of the Choir of the Church of Santa Maria de los Angeles,
Churubusco, Mexico.
Erected in 1678.
Showing Chinese Influence.

57. FAÇADE OF THE CHURCH OF SAN FRANCISCO ACATEPEC,
Near Cholula, Mexico.
Encrusted with Tile Work.

58. PORTION OF ZÓCALO OF THE CHURCH OF SAN FRANCISCO
ACATEPEC,
Near Cholula, Mexico.
Showing Elaborate Tile Work.

Churrigueresque style. The dome is covered with tile-work in various designs with an inscription in bold lettering.

At Celaya, State of Guanajuato, the church of Nuestra del Carmen (1807) has a glazed dome decorated in zigzag pattern with inserted tile panels.

Numerous other churches in Mexico are richly adorned with old Puebla tile designs, including a church at Tepozotlán, near Cuernavaca, but probably the most remarkable example of elaborate tile-work in Mexico is that of the church of San Francisco Acatepec, situated far from any settlement, about five kilometers from Cholula, on the old royal road which runs from Puebla to Atlixco. The façade, tower and belfry of this structure are completely covered with mosaic designs in richly colored enameled tiles. The illustrations show the façade (57) and a tile panel (58) in the *zocalo* at the base to the right of the entrance, above which may be seen a border of six small tiles, each containing the figure of a lamb. The large curved tiles which surround the pillars are especially noteworthy.

The dome of the temple of Nuestra Señora de los Remedios (Our Lady of Remedies) crowning the pyramid of Cholula, near Puebla, is handsomely glazed with colored tile-work.

In many of the cemeteries in the neighborhood of Puebla tiles were used to beautify the graves and tombstones. Some of these, decorated with figures of Saints, may still be observed in place (see illustration 42).

Curved, unglazed roofing tiles, of Spanish form, are still to be seen on buildings in Tasco, Cuernavaca and other places in Mexico.

Maturin M. Ballou, in his *"Aztec Land"* (1890), states that there were in that year eight or ten tile factories in Puebla.

X. Marks on Mexican Maiolica.

As we have already seen, the members of the potters'
guild in Puebla were required to use a clearly marked stamp
or monogram on all pottery made by them after the year
1653. This rule remained in force at least as late as 1676.
It is to be presumed that all pieces of pottery made during
these twenty-three years, when large quantities of the ware
must have been produced, bore some distinguishing mark.
Previous to the organization of the guild the marking of
the ware was not compulsory and we have no knowledge
that the practice was general after the year 1676. We
would, therefore, expect to find among the older pieces of
maiolica a fair percentage bearing trade-marks, which would
indicate the third quarter of the seventeenth century as the
period of manufacture, but in reality marked pieces are ex-
ceedingly rare at the present time. It is not probable that
the stringent laws of the guild should have been ignored
by the potters, and we can only account for the scarcity of
marked examples by the supposition that the great majority
of the earlier pieces have disappeared through breakage or
loss. An occasional piece, however, is found which bears
one or more letters, or a monogram, presumably the initials
or private symbol of the maker or decorator. Of many hundreds of pieces examined by the writer, in public collections
and in private hands, not more than a score or so, exclusive
of tiles, have been found to possess distinguishing marks.

F The mark most frequently found is the letter F,
which is painted in blue on tiles with figure and animal
paintings in combined Spanish and Chinese styles,
which were evidently produced at a single factory. It invariably occurs on the painted side, having been penciled

98

wherever it could be introduced among the decorative designs. In the collection of Mr. Albert Pepper are numerous animal tiles bearing this mark, and others are owned by this Museum (see illustration 41).

On other tiles from the same factory we frequently find the figure of a bee, painted in blue, probably standing for the initial letter of the name of the decorator (see fifth tile in illustration 41). Mr. Albert Pepper has many tiles bearing this device, which he has set in the walls of his residence, near San Angel, a suburb of the City of Mexico.

The large bacino, or bowl, shown in illustration 23, which is ornamented in blue, with brown outlines, in Chinese taste, bears on the under side the letters C. S., painted in the enamel in blue. It is probable that these are the transposed initials of Diego Salvador Carreto, a prominent member of the guild.

A large vase in the Museum collection, decorated in Chinese style (shown in illustration 20), bears on one side a monogram or character in blue, apparently intended for the letters *h e*, or *H e*. This same mark appears on a jar, ten and a half inches high, decorated in blue in the Spanish tattooed style, owned by Mr. Albert Pepper. Could this be the mark of Damian Hernandez, one of the first Inspectors of the potters' guild?

It will be noticed that all of the marked pieces thus far discovered belong evidently to the latter half of the seventeenth century.

In the absence of a complete list of the members of the potters' guild, the exact significance of these marks has not yet been determined.

XI. Forgeries and Reproductions.

As has already been stated there are now six factories in Puebla where ordinary tin enameled pottery is being made in commercial quantities. Similar ware, but of darker red body, is also being produced at Oaxaca. As a rule, the modern Puebla ware is made of rather coarse clay and decorated with rude geometrical designs in various colors,— blue, red, green, yellow, brown, etc. This rude maiolica may be found in the markets in the City of Mexico and the nearby towns, in Puebla and its vicinity.

There is a class of ware, however, which is being fabricated in the city of Puebla, which is of a more dubious character. To supply the demand for ancient maiolica, enterprising manufacturers are now turning out some dangerous counterfeits of the old blue and white wares of the eighteenth century. By the use of a creamy enamel, the chipping of the edges, the artificial tinting of the exposed body, and the grinding of the bases to represent wear, an appearance of age is imparted which is likely to deceive anyone but an expert. The writer has seen several of these pieces in the form of drug jars, which were offered for sale at high prices, in some instances by reputable and honest dealers, who themselves had been deceived. These forgeries can readily be detectd by the pronounced yellowish tint of the ground enamel, which deep color is not found in genuine pieces, and by the smeary appearance of the dark blue pigment, which, instead of having been applied boldly and standing out smoothly and clearly in relief, has been painted roughly and unevenly by numerous strokes of the brush. A

59. GROUP OF MODERN MAIOLICA.
Decorated in Blue.
By Señor Enrique L. Ventosa, of Puebla, Mexico.

comparison of genuine and forged pieces will reveal a marked difference and save the collector from future humiliation. The most misleading feature of these counterfeits is the intentional chipping of the edges and the treatment of the breaks to imitate the staining acquired by great age. Purchasers of Puebla maiolica are cautioned to be on their guard against the acquisition of these more than worthless pieces. Far better to buy an honest modern reproduction, such as those decorated by Señor Ventosa (see illustration 59), which stands for exactly what it is, than to pay a high price for probably a still more recent piece, posing as an antique.

Another variety of ware is being manufactured, which, to the uninitiated, is scarcely less deceptive. We refer to large pieces decorated in Chinese style, having irregular medallions in which are depicted scenes from Aztec and Hispano-Mexican history. We have seen large vases of this character bearing poorly painted and weakly colored figure scenes relating to the Conquest, sometimes accompanied by descriptive inscriptions. While these pieces, to which reference was made in Chapter V, have been supposed to be of the seventeenth century, they are in reality of quite recent manufacture. Illustration 60 will give a fair idea of these recent fabrications.

A third class of ware which is found abundantly in Mexico, examples of which may be seen in almost every collection of Mexican maiolica, is that produced during the second half of the nineteenth century. It is almost invariably painted in polychrome and belongs to the fourth style, which we have classed as Hispano-Mexican, or Pueblan. Large vases, bowls, barrel-shaped jardinieres, jars, cylindrical vessels with flaring mouths surmounted by lids (resembling the modern china toilet slop jars), plates, and other articles, elaborately ornamented with gaudy colorings, are to be

found in every curiosity shop in Mexico, where they pose as
genuine antiques. A careful examination of such pieces will

60. MODERN MAIOLICA VASE.
Decorated in Blue.
Imitating Early Puebla Work.

reveal the fact that the enamel is new and fresh, showing no
signs of age, save where the base rims have been ground to

make them stand evenly and firmly. We find on these pieces no scratches or chipping acquired by long use. While this ware can scarcely be placed in the category of forgeries, since it has probably not been made to deceive the unwary, pieces are nevertheless bought and sold extensively as antiques, although they bear little resemblance to the wares produced prior to the nineteenth century.

There are always to be found in the older wares well-marked characteristics which will enable the collector or student to distinguish them unerringly from their modern imitations. The beautiful quality of the glaze, the deep, rich, tone of the blue enamel, the mellowness of surface imparted by the hand of time, the peculiarities of decorative treatment and the unmistakable evidence of long use, have never been successfully imitated by the modern potters. The later wares possess a hard appearance of body and enamel, a thinness and weakness of coloring, or, when applied thickly, a rawness and freshness of tint, a lack of grace in their lines, and, as a rule, an absence of time cracks and evidences of natural wear, which stamp them, in the eyes of the connoisseur, as present day fabrications, or as bungling frauds.

XII. Recapitulation.

From the meagre references to the pottery industry, found in the early literature of Mexico and the manuscript archives of the City of Puebla, combined with the results of a careful study of the ancient maiolica and tile-work which have survived, we learn that previous to the year 1580 Spanish potters were plying their trade in Mexico and instructing the natives in the mysteries of the art. The first Spanish clay-worker in the New World initiated the Mexicans into the secret of glazing the ware with tin and oxide of lead. Two distinct influences were at work on the ceramic art in New Spain, first the Spanish, through the potters of Talavera, and later the Chinese, through the extensive importation of Oriental porcelains during the seventeenth and eighteenth centuries. The manufacture seems to have been confined to the City of Puebla until a recent period, when potteries were established in Oaxaca for the production of ordinary commercial ware.*

The manufacture of decorative tiles was commenced at an early date, probably before 1575, as is clearly proved by the extensive use of tile-work in many of the oldest churches and convents in New Spain.

Until 1653, in which year a potters' guild was organized, the maiolica and tile industries flourished in Puebla without restriction and during this time, when no guild regulations were in force, a great variety of styles was developed,

---

* At the present time rude pottery glazed with tin, is being produced in Guatamala. A collection of this ware may be seen in the Philadelphia Commercial Museum.

which distinguished the products of individual establishments. The laws which were adopted regulated the careful
preparation of the clays and glazes, the composition of the
ware, and the character of the decorations, and required the
stamping of each piece by the individual mark of the potter. It would seem that this last requirement was enforced
during the existence of the guild, which so far as the archives
show, continued from 1653 to about 1676. After the latter date the organization seems to have languished and the
regulations for the protection of the potters were apparently
no longer enforced. About the middle of the eighteenth
century the decadence set in and the art began rapidly
to decline. About the middle of the nineteenth century
it had reached its lowest ebb. The golden age of the art
appears to have been from about 1650 to 1750.

The earliest maiolica and tiles made in Mexico were
probably decorated in blue, but other colors were introduced
about 1650, as in the rules of the guild, regulating the production of fine ware, in the Talavera style, it was specified
that the figures and designs should be in colors, shaded
with "all the five colors used in the art." These colors
were blue, green, yellow, brown, and red. After the opening of the nineteenth century other colors, such as rose,
purple, etc., were added and a native Mexican or Pueblan
style was developed, in which the early Spanish and Chinese
influences gradually disappeared.

It is not quite clear what was meant by "relief work
in blue." Among the early pieces which have survived we
have found no examples with modeled or moulded decorations in which the body or paste stands out above the surface. A spherical jar bearing around its upper half a few
conventional leaf ornaments (see illustration 61), which, at
first glance, might be taken for relief decoration, on close
inspection proves to have been painted with a brush. The

so-called "relief work" was produced by the thick, viscous, heavily applied blue enamel, which is perceptibly raised above the ground, which effect is so characteristic of the wares of that period, and later. As has been previously stated, however, some of the tile-work was ornamented in embossed patterns (see border at right hand side of illustration 49)

61.   MAIOLICA VASE (12½ Inches in Height).
Decorated in Raised Blue, Outlined in Black.
Puebla, About 1700.
In the Museum Collection.

and a tile in the Museum collection possesses a design modeled in high relief, covered with brilliant tones of yellow and green enamel.

It has only been within the past few years that the Mexicans themselves have begun to recognize the true character of the tin enameled pottery found in their country. Collectors in various parts of the Republic have, as a result of these discoveries, turned their attention to the gathering together and preservation of these interesting remains of an ancient art, and we may look for the formation, in the near future, of more or less important collections. In the meanwhile that which has been secured for this Museum, including a series of decorated tiles consisting of upwards of three hundred of the best designs and patterns, produced from the earliest times to the middle of the nineteenth century, will continue to be the most representative one accessible to ceramic students.

INDEX